THE PALESTINIAN MANNA TRADITION

INSTITUTUM IUDAICUM, TÜBINGEN

OTTO MICHEL

ARBEITEN ZUR GESCHICHTE DES SPÄTEREN JUDENTUMS UND DES URCHRISTENTUMS

BAND VII

THE PALESTINIAN MANNA TRADITION

LEIDEN

E. J. BRILL

1968

THE PALESTINIAN MANNA TRADITION

THE MANNA TRADITION IN THE PALESTINIAN
TARGUMS AND ITS RELATIONSHIP
TO THE NEW TESTAMENT WRITINGS

BY

BRUCE J. MALINA

LEIDEN
E. J. BRILL
1968

TABLE OF CONTENTS

PREFACE

The present work was presented as a dissertation in the year 1967 to the Biblical Faculty of the Institutum Biblicum Franciscanum, in Jerusalem, H.K. Jordan. It is a study of the manna tradition, especially as found in the Palestinian Targums. The theme itself was suggested by the problems raised in a seminar on Jn 6, under Fr. Maximillian Zerwick, S.J., at the Pontifical Biblical Institute, Rome. The problems entailed the value of the use of rabbinic parallels to Jn 6 when these parallels, for the most part, are either undated or undatable, or clearly postdate the N.T. writings, yet are used nevertheless to shed light on the N.T.

For clarity's sake, the following methodological presuppositions have been adopted in this study:

(1) That Biblical traditions regarding Israel's origins were continually re-interpreted for the benefit of the community both before and after these traditions were consigned to writing in the canonical books;

(2) That this process of re-interpretation can often be adequately traced;

(3) That the understanding of Israel's traditions as manifested in the N.T. naturally depends upon the stage of re-interpretation extant at the time;

(4) That to understand the N.T. conceptions of Israel's traditions, it is necessary to investigate the evidence and clearly define what level of interpretation would probably have been part of the N.T. milieu;

(5) That the historical probability of a re-interpreted O.T. tradition's being part of the N.T. milieu (i.e. evidence of existence at the same time and place) is valid and suffices for the understanding of the background of the N.T.; and if the N.T. evidence warrants it, an attempt at demonstrating the factual use of a given O.T. re-interpretation in the N.T. should be made;

(6) That the mere possibility of a relationship (i.e. lack of clear-cut time and place evidence of relationship) between an O.T. re-interpretation and the N.T. is valueless for added insight into the N.T. background. Such "parallels" only confuse the issue and discourage further research.

The purpose of this study is to present the evidence concerning the idea of the manna in vogue in N.T. times in Palestine. To attain this end we have deemed it appropriate to study the extant Palestinian Targums, which mirror the then current re-interpretations of the O.T. traditions to a goodly extent. This last statement naturally requires some bolstering, which would normally have been the burden of an introduction to this work. However since two recent works (R. Le Déaut, *La nuit pascale*: *Essai sur la signification de la Pâque juive à partir du Targum d'Exode XII*, 42 (Analecta Biblica 22; Rome 1963), 41-71; and M. McNamara, *The New Testament and the Palestinian Targum to the Pentateuch* (Analecta Biblica 27; Rome, 1966), 5-66) have adequately and admirably dealt with the question of the value and function of the Palestinian Targums in N.T. research, we feel we can dispense with the introductory questions, leaving the reader to consult the aforementioned works, and proceed directly to the problem at hand.

Any study of targumic traditions presupposes a thorough study of the O.T. texts from which these traditions derive. Hence in the first chapter of our study, we consider the O.T. texts dealing with the manna, with a view to tracing the tradition of the O.T. to the time of the last canonical Palestinian writings. In the second chapter, we present the texts of the Palestinian Targums in translation, and then attempt to determine whether the manna traditions in these Targums are late additions or ancient bits of exegesis already extant in N.T. times, a period we designate pre-mishnaic. In the final chapter, we compare the results of our study of the manna tradition in the Palestinian Targums and the relevant N.T. texts.

Leaving aside the majestic "we" of scholarly style, I gratefully acknowledge my debt of gratitude to Fr. Roger Le Déaut, C.S.Sp., of the Pontifical Biblical Institute, for his kindness, encouragement, erudition and guidance. Further thanks are due to my Franciscan confreres, Frs. Elpidius Pax, PhD., S. T. D., Director of the Studium Biblicum Franciscanum; Emmanuel Miguéns, S. T. D., S. S. D., faculty advisor for this work; and Benjamin Baran, A. B., S. T. L., who read this work in manuscript and offered helpful suggestions. And finally, I must add a note of thanks to the Society for the Propagation of the Faith, Brooklyn, N.Y., for providing me with a subsidy for the pursuit of Biblical studies at Rome and Jerusalem.

Studium Biblicum Franciscanum   Bruce J. MALINA, O.F.M.
Jerusalem
February 2, 1967

BIBLIOGRAPHY

(With Abbreviations)

I. SOURCES (INCLUDING TRANSLATIONS)

A. *Biblical Texts and Versions*

Biblia Hebraica, ed. R. Kittel, 7th ed. by P. Kahle, A. Alt, O. Eissfeldt. Stuttgart, 1951.

Biblia Polyglotta Matritensia, Series IV: Targum Palaestinense in Pentateuchum, ed. A. Díez Macho. Madrid, 1965 (sample copy).

Biblia Sacra Polyglotta, 6 vols., ed. B. Walton. London, 1653-1657.

The Bible in Aramaic: I. The Pentateuch according to Targum Onkelos; II. The Former Prophets according to Targum Jonathan; III. The Latter Prophets according to Targum Jonathan, ed. A. Sperber. Leiden, 1959-1962.

Codex Neofiti I, Vatican Library.

Das Fragmententhargum (Thargum jeruschalmi zum Pentateuch), ed. M. Ginsburger. Berlin, 1899.

MS 607 (ENA 2576), Jewish Theological Seminary of New York, ed. A. Díez Macho, "Un nuevo Targum a los Profetas," Estudios Biblicos, 15 (1956), 293-295.

The Old Testament in Greek, 3 vols., ed. H. B. Swete. 4th ed. Cambridge, 1909-1912.

Septuaginta, 2 vols., ed. A. Rahlfs. Stuttgart, 1935.

Novum Testamentum graece et latine, ed. A. Merk. 8th ed. Rome, 1957.

B. *Non-Rabbinic Texts and Versions*

Charles, R. H., The Apocrypha and Pseudepigrapha of the Old Testament in English. 2 vols. Oxford, 1913.

Funk, F. X., Opera Patrum Apostolicorum. 2 vols. Tübingen, 1887.

Riessler, P., Altjüdisches Schrifttum ausserhalb der Bibel. Augsburg, 1928.

Aphraates, Demonstrationes, ed. R. Graffin, Patrologia Syriaca I. Paris, 1894.

Irenaeus, Fragmenta deperditorum operum, PG VII, 1225-1264.

Josephus: Flavii Iosephi Opera, 6 vols., ed. B. Niese. Berlin, 1887-1895.

Liber Apocalypseos Baruch Filii Neriae, ed. M. Kmosko: in R. Graffin (ed.). Patrologia Syriaca II. Paris, 1907, 1056-1237.

Memar Marqah: the Teaching of Marqah, ed. J. MacDonald, (Beihefte zur ZAW 84/I-II). Berlin, 1963.

Die Oracula Sibyllina, ed. J. Geffcken, (Die griechischen christlichen Schriftsteller der ersten drei Jahrhunderte 8). Leipzig, 1902.

Philonis Alexandri Opera quae supersunt, 6 vols., ed. L. Cohn - P. Wendland (editio minor). Berlin, 1896-1915.

Pseudo-Philo: The Biblical Antiquities of Philo, trans. and notes by M. R. James. London, 1917.

The Scroll of the War of the Sons of Light against the Sons of Darkness, trans. and notes by Y. Yadin. Oxford, 1962.

Theophilus of Antioch, Ad Autolycum, PG VI, 1023-1168.

The Zadokite Documents, ed. C. Rabin. 2d ed. Oxford, 1958.

C. *Rabbinic Texts and Versions*

Aboth de Rabbi Nathan, ed. S. Schechter. Vienna, 1887.

The Fathers according to Rabbi Nathan, trans. and notes by J. Goldin, (Yale Judaica Series X). New Haven, 1955.

Mechilta d'Rabbi Ismael cum variis lectionibus et adnotationibus, ed. H. S. Horovitz with I. A. Rabin, (Corpus tannaiticum III/1). Frankfurt, 1931.

Midrash Leqaḥ Ṭob = R. Tobiah b. R. Eliezer (d. after 1107): in B. Ugolino, Thesaurus Antiquitatum Sacrarum, XVI, 997-1226. Venice, 1753; and XVII. Venice, 1754.

The Midrash on Psalms, trans. and notes by W. G. Braude, (Yale Judaica Series XIII/1-2). New Haven, 1959.

Midrash Rabbah, 10 vols., ed. H. Freedman and M. Simon. 2d ed. London, 1951·
   Exodus, trans. and notes by S. M. Lehrmann. Vol. III.
   Leviticus, trans. and notes by J. Israelstam and J. J. Slotki. Vol. IV.
   Numbers, trans. and notes by J. J. Slotki. Vol. V-VI.
   Deuteronomy, trans. and notes by J. Rabbinowitz. Vol. VII.
   Ecclesiastes, trans. and notes by A. Cohen. Vol. VIII.
   Song of Songs, trans. and notes by M. Simon. Vol. IX.

Midrash Tanḥuma, ed. Ḥ. Zundel (?). Jerusalem, 1960.

The Mishnah, trans. and notes by H. Danby. Oxford, 1933.
   Berakot (Gebete), ed. O. Holtzmann: in G. Beer and O. Holtzmann (eds.), Die Mischna I/1. Giessen, 1912.
   Schabbat (Sabbat), ed. W. Nowack: in G. Beer, O. Holtzmann and I. Rabin (eds.), Die Mischna II/1. Giessen, 1924.
   Abot (Väter), ed. K. Marti and G. Beer: in G. Beer and O. Holtzmann (eds.), Die Mischna IV/9. Giessen, 1927.

Rashi: M. Rosenbaum and A. M. Silbermann, Pentateuch with Targum Onkelos, Haphtaroth and Prayers for Sabbath and Rashi's Commentary, 5 vols. London, 1929-1934.

Seder Eliahu rabba und Seder Eliahu zuta, ed. L. M. Friedmann. Vienna, 1902.

Sifré debé Rab: der älteste halachische und hagadische Midrasch zu Numeri und Deuteronomium, ed. M. Friedmann. Vienna, 1864.

Siphre ad numeros adjecto Siphre zutta, ed. H. S. Horovitz, (Corpus tannaiticum III/3). Leipzig, 1917.

Talmud: Le Talmud de Jérusalem, trans. and notes by M. Schwab. 11 vols. Paris, 1932-1933.

The Babylonian Talmud, ed. I. Epstein. The 18 volume edition. London, 1961·
   Berakoth, trans. and notes by M. Simon. Zeraʿim.
   ʿErubin, trans. and notes by I. Slotki. Moʿed II.
   Pesaḥim, trans. and notes by H. Freedman. Moʿed II.
   Yoma, trans. and notes by L. Jung. Moʿed III.
   Sukkah, trans. and notes by I. Slotki. Moʿed III.
   Taʿanith, trans. and notes by J. Rabbinowitz. Moʿed IV.
   Megillah, trans. and notes by M. Simon. Moʿed IV.
   Ḥagigah, trans. and notes by I. Abrahams. Moʿed IV.
   Soṭah, trans. and notes by A. Cohen. Nashim III.
   Sanhedrin, trans. and notes by J. Schachter and M. Freedman. Nezikin III.
   Aboth, trans. and notes by J. Israelstam. Nezikin IV.
   ʿArakin, trans. and notes by L. Jung. Ḳodashim III.

Tosephta, based on the Erfurt and Vienna Codices, ed. M. S. Zuckermandel. Reprint: Jerusalem, 1963.

II. LITERATURE

Allo, E. B. Saint Jean: L'Apocalypse. (EB) Paris, 1921.

——. Saint Paul: Première épitre aux Corinthiens. (EB) Paris, 1934.

Alonso-Schökel, L. Genera litteraria: Annotationes in usum alumnorum. Mimeographed. Rome, 1965.

Auzou, G. De la servitude au service. Paris, 1961.

Bachmann, P. Der erste Brief des Paulus an die Korinther. (Kommentar zum N.T. ed. T. Zahn) Leipzig, 1921.

Barth, C. "Zur Bedeutung der Wüstentradition," Volume du Congrès: Genève, 1965. (Supplements to Vetus Testamentum XV; Leiden, 1966), 14-23.

Barthélemy, D. Les devanciers d'Aquila: Première publication intégrale du texte des fragments du Dodécaprophéton trouvés dans le désert de Juda, précédée d'une étude sur les traductions et recensions grecques de la Bible réalisées au premier siècle de notre ère sous l'influence du rabbinat palestinien. (Supplements to Vetus Testamentum X) Leiden, 1963.

Benoit, P. "Paulinisme et Johannisme," NTS, 9 (1962/1963), 193-207.

Beyerlin, W. Origins and History of the Oldest Sinaitic Traditions, trans. S. Rudman. Oxford, 1965.

Billerbeck, P. Kommentar zum Neuen Testament aus Talmud und Midrasch. 4 vols. Munich, 1922-1928.

Bloch, R. "Ezéchiel XVI: exemple parfait du procédé midrashique dans la Bible," Cahiers Sioniens, 9 (1955), 193-223.

——. "Midrash," DBS, V, 1263-1281.

——. "Note méthodologique pour l'étude de la littérature rabbinique," RSR, 43 (1955), 194-227.

——. "Quelques aspects de la figure de Moïse dans la tradition rabbinique," Moïse, l'homme de l'Alliance. Paris, 1955. 91-167.

Blau, L. "Baṭ Ḳol," The Jewish Encyclopedia. New York, 1903. II, 588-592.

Boismard, M. E. L'Apocalypse. (Bible de Jérusalem) Paris, 1950.

——. "Les Citations targumique dans le quatrième évangile," Revue Biblique, 66 (1959), 374-378.

Bonsirven, G. L'Apocalisse di San Giovanni, trans. U. Massi. (Verbum Salutis) Rome, 1963.

Borgen, P. Bread from Heaven: an Exegetical Study of the Concept of Manna in the Gospel of John and the Writings of Philo. (Supplements to Novum Testamentum X) Leiden, 1965.

Brekelmans, C. "Die sogenannten deuteronomistischen Elemente in Genesis bis Numeri: ein Beitrag zur Vorgeschichte des Deuteronomiums," Volume du Congrès: Genève 1965. (Supplements to Vetus Testamentum XV; Leiden, 1966), 90-96.

Brockington, L. H. "Septuagint and Targum," ZAW, 66 (1954), 80-86.

Brown, R. E. The Gospel according to John I-XII. (Anchor Bible 29) New York, 1966.

Buchanan, G. W. "Eschatology and the 'End of Days'," Journal of Near Eastern Studies, 20 (1961), 188-193.

Büchler, A. "The Reading of the Law and the Prophets in a Triennial Cycle," Jewish Quarterly Review, 5 (1893), 420-468; 6 (1894), 1-73.

Buxtorf Jr., J. "Historia Arcae Foederis," in B. Ugolino (ed.), Thesaurus Antiquitatum Sacrarum. Venice, 1747. VIII, 143-350.

Buxtorf Sr., J. "Dissertatio de Manna," in B. Ugolino (ed.), Thesaurus Antiquitatum Sacrarum. Venice, 1747. VIII, 587-640.

——. Lexicon Chaldaicum, Talmudicum et Rabbinicum. Basel, 1640.

Catford, J. C. A Linguistic Theory of Translation: an Essay in Applied Linguistic s. London, 1965.

Cazelles, H. "Pentateuque: IV. Le nouveau 'status quaestionis'," DBS, VII, 736-858.

——. "Sur les origines du calendrier des Jubilés," Biblica, 43 (1962), 202-212.

Charles, R. H. A Critical and Exegetical Commentary on the Revelation of St. John. Vol. I. (ICC) Edinburgh, 1920.

Cohn, L. "An Apocryphal Work Ascribed to Philo of Alexandria," Jewish Quarterly Review, 10 (1898), 277-332.

Coppens, J. "Les traditions relatives à la manne dans Exode XVI," Estudios Eclesiásticos, 34 (1960), 473-489.

Daube, D. "The Earliest Structure of the Gospels," NTS, 5 (1958/1959), 174-187.

De Vaux, R. Ancient Israel: Its Life and Institutions, trans. J. McHugh. London, 1961.

Díez Macho, A. "Un nuevo Targum a los Profetas," Estudios Biblicos, 15 (1956), 287-295.

——. "The Recently Discovered Palestinian Targum: Its Antiquity and Relationship with the Other Targums," Congress Volume: Oxford. (Supplements to Vetus Testamentum VII; Leiden, 1960), 222-245.

——. "Targum," Enciclopedia de la Biblia. Barcelona, 1965. VI, 865-881.

Driver, S. R. A Critical and Exegetical Commentary on Deuteronomy. (ICC) Edinburgh, 1902.

Düsterdieck, F. Kritisch exegetisches Handbuch über die Offenbarung Johannis. (Meyer's Kritisch exegetischer Kommentar über das N.T.) Göttingen, 1887.

Eissfeldt, O. Hexateuch-Synopse. 2d ed. Darmstadt, 1962.

——. The Old Testament: an Introduction, trans. P. Ackroyd. London, 1965.

Fichtner, J. Weisheit Salomos. (Handbuch zum alten Testament) Tübingen, 1938.

Findlay, G. G. St Paul's First Epistle to the Corinthians: in W. R. Nicoll (ed.), The Expositor's Greek Testament. London, 1900. II, 727-953.

Finkel, A. The Pharisees and the Teacher of Nazareth. (Arbeiten zur Geschichte des Spätjudentums und Urchristentums 4) Leiden, 1964.

Ford, J. M. "The First Epistle to the Corinthians or the First Epistle to the Hebrews?," CBQ, 28 (1966) 402-416.

Gärtner, B. John VI and the Jewish Passover. (Coniectanea N.T. 17) Uppsala, 1959.

Geiger, A. Urschrift und Übersetzungen der Bibel in ihrer Abhängigkeit von der innern Entwicklung des Judentums. 2d ed. Frankfurt/M., 1928.

George, A. "Les Récits de Gilgal en Josué (V, 2-15)," Memorial J. Chaine. (Bibliothèque de la Faculté Catholique de Théologie de Lyon 5) Lyon, 1950. 169-186.

Gerhardsson, B. Memory and Manuscript: Oral Tradition and Written Transmission in Rabbinic Judaism and Early Christianity, trans. E. J. Sharpe. (Acta Seminarii Neotestamentici Uppsaliensis 22) Lund-Copenhagen, 1961.

Ginzberg, L. The Legends of the Jews. 6 vols. and indices. Philadelphia, 1909-1928.

Goppelt, L. "Paulus und die Heilsgeschichte: Schlussfolgerungen aus Röm. IV und I. Kor. X. 1-13," NTS, 13 (1966/1967), 31-47.

——. "πόμα, πόσις, ποτόν, πότος," TWNT, VI, 145-148.

Gray, G. B. A Critical and Exegetical Commentary on Numbers. (ICC) Edinburgh, 1903.

Gray, J. "The Desert Sojourn of the Hebrews and the Sinai-Horeb Tradition," VT, 4 (1954), 148-154.

Grelot, P. " 'De son ventre couleront des fleuves d'eau,' la citation Scripturaire de Jean VII, 38," Revue Biblique, 66 (1959), 369-374.

Guilding, A. The Fourth Gospel and Jewish Worship: a Study of the Relation of St. John's Gospel to the Ancient Jewish Lectionary System. Oxford, 1960.

Guttmann, A. "The Significance of Miracles for Talmudic Judaism," HUCA, 20 (1947), 363-406.

Haenchen, E. " 'Der Vater, der mich gesandt hat'," NTS, 9 (1962/1963), 208-216.

Hatch, E. and Redpath, H. A Concordance to the Septuagint. 2 vols. Reprint. Graz, 1954.

Heinrici, G. Kritisch exegetisches Handbuch über den ersten Brief an die Korinther. (Meyer's Kritisch exegetischer Kommentar über N.T.) Göttingen, 1888.

Herrmann, W. "Götterspeise und Göttertrank in Ugarit und Israel," ZAW, 72 (1960), 205-216.

Jastrow, M. A Dictionary of the Targumim, the Talmud Babli and Yerushalmi and the Midrashic Literature. 2 vols. New York, 1950.

Jaubert, A. La Date de la Cène. (EB) Paris, 1957.

Junker, H. "Die Entstehungszeit des Ps 78 und das Deuteronomium," Biblica, 34 (1953), 487-500.

Kahle, P. "Das palästinische Pentateuchtargum und das zur Zeit Jesu gesprochene Aramäisch," ZNW, 49 (1958), 100-116.

Käsemann, E. "Anliegen und Eigenart der paulinischen Abendmahlslehre," Evangelische Theologie, 7 (1947/1948), 263-283: in Essays on New Testament Themes, trans. W. J. Montague. (Studies in Biblical Theology 41) London, 1964. 108-135.

Kimbrough Jr., S. T. "The Concept of Sabbath at Qumran," Revue de Qumran, 5 (1966), 483-502.

Kraus, H. J. Psalmen I-II. (Biblischer Kommentar Altes Testament XV) Neukirchen, 1961.

——. Worship in Israel, trans. G. Buswell. Oxford, 1966.

Kruse, H. "Die 'dialektische Negation' als semitisches Idiom," VT, 4 (1954), 385-400.

Kutsch, E. "Erwägungen zur Geschichte der Passafeier und des Massotfestes," Zeitschrift für Theologie und Kirche, 55 (1958), 1-35.

——. "Der Kalender des Jubiläenbuches und das Alte und das Neue Testament," VT, 11 (1961), 39-47.

——. "מִקְרָא," ZAW, 65 (1953), 247-253.

Le Déaut, R. Introduction à la littérature targumique. Première partie. Rome, 1966.

——. "Miryam, soeur de Moïse, et Marie, mère du Messie," Biblica, 45 (1964), 198-219.

——. La nuit pascale: Essai sur la signification de la Pâque juive à partir du Targum d'Exode XII, 42. (Analecta Biblica 22) Rome, 1963.

——. "Le Targum de Gen 22, 8 et 1 Pt 1, 20," RSR, 49 (1961), 103-106.

Lehmann, O. "Aggadah," Enciclopedia de la Biblia. Barcelona, 1963. I, 213-219.

Levy, J. Chaldäisches Wörterbuch über die Targumim und einen grossen Theil des rabbinischen Schriftums. Reprint. Cologne, 1959.

Lohfink, N. Das Hauptgebot: eine Untersuchung literarischer Einleitungsfragen zu Dtn. 5-11. (Analecta Biblica 20) Rome, 1963.

McNamara, M. The New Testament and the Palestinian Targum to the Pentateuch. (Analecta Biblica 27) Rome, 1966.

——. "Targumic Studies," CBQ, 28 (1966), 1-19.

Mandelkern, S. Veteris Testamenti Concordantiae. 2 vols. Reprint. Graz, 1937.

Martelet, G. "Sacrements, figures et exhortation en I Cor. X, 1-11," RSR, 44 (1956), 323-359; 515-559.

Mauser, U. W. Christ in the Wilderness. (Studies in Biblical Theology 39) London, 1963.
Moffat, J. The Revelation of St. John the Divine: in W. R. Nicoll (ed.), The Expositor's Greek Testament. London, 1910. V, 279-494.
Morgenstern, J. "The Chanukkah Festival and the Calendar of Ancient Israel," HUCA, 20 (1947), 1-136.
Morris, L. The New Testament and the Jewish Lectionaries. London, 1964.
Mowinckel, S. The Psalms in Israel's Worship II, trans. D. R. Ap-Thomas. New York, 1962.
Myers, J. M. Ezra-Nehemia. (Anchor Bible 14) New York, 1965.
Neuenzeit, P. Das Herrenmahl: Studien zur paulinischen Eucharistieauffassung. (Studien zum A.T. und N.T. 1) Munich, 1960.
Noth, M. Exodus: A Commentary, trans. J. S. Bowden. (Old Testament Library) London, 1962.
———. Das Buch Josua. (Handbuch zum Alten Testament) 2d ed. Tübingen, 1953.
———. "Num. 21 als Glied der 'Hexateuch'-Erzählung," ZAW, 58 (1940/1941), 161-189.
———. Überlieferungsgeschichte des Pentateuch. Stuttgart, 1948.
———. Überlieferungsgeschichtliche Studien. 2d ed. Tübingen, 1957.
Oepke, A. "κρύπτω," TWNT, III, 959-979.
Prigent, P. Apocalypse et Liturgie. (Cahiers Theologiques 52) Neuchatel, 1964.
Rabbinowitz, J. Mishnah Megillah. London, 1931.
Ramsay, W. M. The Letters to the Seven Churches of Asia and their Place in the Plan of the Apocalypse. London, 1904.
Robertson, A. and Plummer, A. A Critical and Exegetical Commentary on the First Epistle of St. Paul to the Corinthians. (ICC) 2d ed. Edinburgh, 1914.
Rowley, H. H. "The Suffering Servant and the Davidic Messiah," Oudtestamentische Studiën, 8 (1950), 100-136.
Ruckstuhl, E. Chronology of the Last Days of Jesus, trans. V. Drapela. New York, 1965.
Rudolph, W. Ezra und Nehemia samt 3. Ezra. (Handbuch zum Alten Testament) Tübingen, 1949.
Sandmel, S. "The Haggada within Scripture," JBL, 80 (1961), 105-122.
Schweizer, E. "πνεῦμα, πνευματικός," TWNT, VI, 387-450.
Seeligmann, I. L. "Voraussetzungen der Midraschexegese," Congress Volume: Copenhagen 1953. (Supplements to Vetus Testamentum I; Leiden, 1953), 150-181.
Skehan, P. "The Date of the Last Supper," CBQ, 20 (1958), 192-199.
Smith, R. H. "Exodus Typology in the Fourth Gospel," JBL, 81 (1962), 329-342.
Soggin, J. A. "Gilgal, Passah und Landnahme: eine neue Untersuchung des kultischen Zusammenhangs der Kap. III-VI des Josuabuches," Volume du Congrès: Genève 1965. (Supplements to Vetus Testamentum XV; Leiden, 1966), 263-277.
Sonne, I. "The Paintings of the Dura Synagogue," HUCA, 20 (1947), 255-362.
Spicq, C. Épitre aux Corinthiens. (La Sainte Bible, Pirot-Clamer XI/2) Paris, 1948.
Stenning, J. F. "Targum," Encyclopedia Brittanica. London, 1960. XXI, 810-812.
Strack, H. L. and Billerbeck, P.: see under Billerbeck.
Swete, H. B. The Apocalypse of St. John. 3d ed. London, 1922.
Te Stroete, G. Exodus. (De Boeken van het Oude Testament I/II) Roermond en Maaseik, 1966.
Thackeray, H. St. John. Josephus IV. Jewish Antiquities I-IV. (The Loeb Classical Library) London, 1957.

Torczyner, H. "The Firmament and the Clouds: Rāqîa and Shehāqîm," Studia Theologica, 1 (1947), 187-196.
Torrey, C. C. "The Messiah Son of Ephraim," JBL, 66 (1947), 253-277.
Vella, J. La Giustizia forense di Dio. (Supplementi alla Rivista Biblica I) Brescia, 1964.
Vermes, G. "Haggadah in the Onkelos Targum," Journal of Semitic Studies, 8 (1963), 159-169.
——. Scripture and Tradition in Judaism: Haggadic Studies. (Studia Post-Biblica 4) Leiden, 1961.
——. "The Targumic Versions of Genesis IV, 3-16," The Annual of Leeds University Oriental Society, 3 (1961/1962), 81-114.
Vernet, J. "Calendario Judío," Enciclopedia de la Biblia. Barcelona, 1964. II, 43-46.
——. "Mes," Enciclopedia de la Biblia. Barcelona, 1965. V, 69-71.
Vogt, E. "Note sur le calendrier du Déluge," Biblica, 43 (1962), 212-216.
Vogt, H. C. M. Studie zur nachexilischen Gemeinde in Esra-Nehemia. Werl, 1966.
Von Rad, G. Old Testament Theology I, trans. D. M. G. Stalker. New York, 1962.
——. Studies in Deuteronomy. (Studies in Biblical Theology 9) London, 1953.
Weiser, A. The Psalms, trans. H. Hartwell. (Old Testament Library) London, 1962.
Wernicke, K. "Ambrosia," in F. Pauly- G. Wissowa (eds.), Real-Encyclopädie der classischen Altertumswissenschaft. Stuttgart, 1894. I, 1809-1811.
Wikenhauser, A. Offenbarung des Johannes. (Regensburger N.T.) Regensburg, 1947.
Winter, P. "Lc 2,49 and the Targum Yerushalmi," ZNW, 45 (1954), 145-179.
Wright, A. "The Literary Genre Midrash," CBQ, 28 (1966), 105-138; 417-457.
Zahn, T. Die Offenbarung des Johannes: Erste Hälfte. (Kommentar zum N.T. ed. T. Zahn) Leipzig, 1924.
Ziegler, J. "Die Hilfe Gottes 'am Morgen'," Alttestamentliche Studien Friedrich Nötscher... gewidmet. (Bonner biblische Beiträge I) Bonn, 1950. 281-288.
Zimmerli, W. "Das Wort des göttlichen Selbsterweises (Erweiswort): eine prophetische Gattung," Mélanges bibliques rédigés en l'honneur de A. Robert. (Travaux de l'Institut catholique de Paris 4) n.p., 1957. 154-164.
——. Erkenntnis Gottes nach dem Buch Ezechiel: eine theologische Studie. (Abhandlungen zur Theologie des Alten und Neuen Testaments 27) Zurich, 1954.

III. ABBREVIATIONS

Ant.	= Jewish Antiquities of Flavius Josephus
CBQ	= Catholic Biblical Quarterly
CDC	= The Zadokite Documents
DBS	= Dictionnaire de la Bible — Supplément
EB	= Études Bibliques
HUCA	= Hebrew Union College Annual
ICC	= International Critical Commentary
J.	= Jerusalem (Talmud)
JBL	= Journal of Biblical Literature
LXX	= Septuagint
M.	= Mishnah
MT	= Masoretic Text of the Biblia Hebraica ed. R. Kittel

N   = Codex Neofiti I
NTS   = New Testament Studies
PG   = Patrologia Graeca (-Latina), ed. Migne
PT   = Palestinian Targum(s)
1 QM   = Qumran War Scroll
R.   = (Midrash) Rabbah
RSR   = Récherches de science religieuse
Tg   = Targum
TJI   = Targum of Pseudo-Jonathan
TJII   = Fragmentary Targum
TO   = Targum Onkelos
TWNT   = Theologisches Wörterbuch zum Neuen Testament, ed. G. Kittel
           Stuttgart, 1933 —
VT   = Vetus Testamentum
ZAW   = Zeitschrift für die alttestamentliche Wissenschaft
ZNW   = Zeitschrift für die neutestamentliche Wissenschaft

CHAPTER ONE

THE MANNA TRADITION IN THE OLD TESTAMENT

Any consideration of Palestinian exegesis as contained in the Targums ought naturally begin with a survey of the biblical traditions from which this exegesis takes its point of departure. The tradition of the manna has its biblical record set down in the following passages: Ex 16; Nb 11, 6-9; Nb 21, 5; Dt 8, 3.16; Josh 5, 12; Ps 78, 23-25; Ps 105, 40; Neh 9, 15.20.[1]) Our task in this chapter is to try to trace the development of the manna tradition in these passages.

A. The Manna Tradition in the Hexateuch [2])

1) *Exodus* 16

The first mention of the manna in the biblical narrative comes in Ex 16. A cursory reading of this chapter shows that it abounds in repetitions, has a shifting cast of characters, and is concerned with various focuses of interest. Modern research has offered a host of hypotheses relative to the sources of the elements clustered in this chapter.[3]) Yet upon surveying the many and all too varied opinions of the critics, it seems that the surest course to take is that of Coppens, who would renounce the task of assigning the various verses of Ex 16 to appropriate layers of the classic documentary or tradition hy-

---

[1]) Wis 16, 20-29; 19, 21 likewise records the manna tradition; but since it is not of Palestinian origin, it enters our discussion only indirectly, and we shall make use of it in that way.

[2]) The term "Hexateuch" is taken functionally here, without reference to a theory on the origins of the O.T. corpus.

[3]) See the sampling offered by J. Coppens, "Les Traditions relatives à la manne dans Exode XVI," *Estudios Eclesiásticos* 34 (1960), 473-489, *passim*; as will be seen from this study, the results of our analysis agree substantially with those of Coppens, but they derive from different and possibly more accurate methods. To Coppens' listing we might add: H. Cazelles, "Pentateuque: IV. Le nouveau 'status quaestionis'," *DBS*, VII, cols. 736-858; Cazelles analyzes Ex 16 as follows: J = 4-5, 13b-15, 21b, 27-30 or 29-30, 35b (col. 786); P = 1-3, 6-13a, 16-21a, 22-26, 31?, 32-34, 35a, 36 (col. 833); and more specifically to P^s = 6-7 and 9-10 or 11, 32-34 (col. 847); G. Te Stroete, *Exodus* (De Boeken van het Oude Testament I/II; Roermond en Maaseik, 1966), 118: P = 1-3, 6-12, 16-20, 22-27, 32-35a; J = 4, 13b-15, 21, 31; D = 5, 28; vv 5, 29-30 are disputed, either J (with Noth) or P.

pothesis until completing a critical study of all the narrative sections
of the second book of the Pentateuch.[1])

On the other hand to renounce labelling passages as belonging to
given sources does not mean to renounce the critical study of the
matter at hand with a view to determing the various literary entities
that make it up. As Coppens shows, Ex 16 offers ample opportunity
for such critical study.

a) *The Diverse Literary Entities in Ex 16*

To begin with, we might take note of the varied cast of characters
in the chapter under consideration. The first principals mentioned are
"the whole congregation of the children of Israel," Moses, and Aaron.
They come to the fore in vv 1, 2, 6 (with LXX for *'adat*), 9, 10. Verse 7
is part of the sentence begun in v 6, while v 8 is a doublet of vv 6-7;
hence all three of these verses belong together. Consequently, we
would consider vv 1-2, 6-10 as one narrative, if only because of the
principals involved.

The second set of principals noted are the pair "the children of
Israel" and Moses. "The children of Israel" with or without Moses
are mentioned in vv 3, 12, 15, 17, 31 (with LXX, S and T), 35a.
Verse 3c makes mention of "this whole *qahal*," hence it would seem
to belong to the cast featuring "the whole *'adat* etc." mentioned above.
Verse 11 introduces v 12, while vv 13-14 continue the narration
begun in v 12 and continued in v 15. Verse 17 presupposes a command
or directive, given previously as in v 16; and v 18 is clearly linked
with v 17. Thus simply from the viewpoint of the persons involved,
it would seem that tentatively at least vv 3ab, 11-18, 31, 35a form a
second narrative.

Then there are the passages in which the main actors dominating
the scene are Moses and "they", either together or alone. Prescinding
from the previously ascribed passages, we find Moses alone in v 4
and in v 5 that is part of the same sentence; in vv 19-20; the "he"
implied as the one making the speech of vv 23-24; then explicitly
for the speech of vv 25-29. The "they" figure in vv 21, 30 and 35b.
Hence for the time being, this third narrative would include vv
4-5, 19-30, 35b.

Although Moses alone is mentioned in v 32, yet it seems this verse
does not belong to the previous narrative grouping. The reason for

---

[1]) Coppens, *art. cit.*, 487.

this is that a new pair of principals is mentioned in vv 33-34, namely Moses and Aaron alone, without "the whole congregation of the children of Israel." And since these verses narrate the fulfillment of the command given in v 32, we would consider vv 32-34 as a fourth narrative.

Thus from the viewpoint of the cast of characters involved we have four narratives in Ex 16:

1) Moses, Aaron and the whole congregation: vv 1-2, 3c, 6-10.
2) Moses and the children of Israel: vv 3ab, 11-18, 31, 35a.
3) Moses and they: vv 4-5, 19-30, 35b.
4) Moses and Aaron: vv 32-34.

If there are four narratives interwoven to form our chapter, this fact should be equally borne out by the style and contents of these narratives. A logical place to begin an inquiry into the style and contents of these pieces would be the "Moses and they" narrative since it offers the largest block of uninterrupted material.

Now from the available stylistic indications, it would seem that vv 19-20, 23-24 and 25-30 form literary units.

1) vv 19-20: the structure of this piece is A B 1 2/1′ 2′ B′ A′:

A	Moše
B	ʾalehem
1	command: ʿad boqer
2	result
1′	non-fulfillment of command: ʿad boqer
2′	result
B	ʾalehem
A′	Moše

The contents of this piece: the disobedience of the people.

2) vv 23-24: the structure of this piece: A B/B′ A′ and conclusion:

A	command: wayyomer ʾalehem (i.e. Moses)
B	ʿad-boqer
B′	ʿad-boqer
A′	fulfillment of command: kaʾašer ṣiwwa Moše

Conclusion

The contents of this piece: obedience to the command and beneficial result.

3) vv 25-30: the structure of this piece appears to be based on the days of the week mentioned. Verse 28 does not fit in since it lacks any mention of the key words involved. The structure would be: A 1 2 B C B′ 1′ 2′ A′:

A	šabbat
1	šešet yamîm
2	bayyôm haššᵉbiʿi
B	šabbat
C	bayyôm haššᵉbiʿi
B′	haššabbat
1′	bayyôm haššišši
2′	bayyôm haššᵉbiʿi
A′	wayyišbᵉtû . . . bayyôm haššᵉbiʿi

In a chiastic structure such as this, the point being highlighted is normally the central point, here C. And C, v 27, tells of the disobedience of the people with regard to the Sabbath precept. Hence this passage would underline that disobedience.[1]

Further, v 22 seems to form a literary unit of sorts with v 4aα and v 5. The vocabulary in both passages is quite similar and the mention of "the sixth day" links them over the expanse of the intervening verses of our present Ex 16. The structure would be: A 1 B C/1′ C′ B′ A′:

v 4aα:	A	wayyomer
v 5:	1	bayyôm haššišši
	B	yabî'û
	C	yilqᵉṭû
v 22:	1′	bayyôm haššišši
	C′	laqᵉṭû
	B′	wayyabo'û
	A′	wayyaggîdû

The purpose of the structure would be to link vv 22 ff with v 5. Verses 22 ff would consequently be an explanation or commentary on v 5. The commentary consists of a midrash on the Sabbath, a key word in the section, in two parts: vv 23-24—the obedience of the people; and vv 25-27. 29-30 — the disobedience of the people.

---

[1] Verse 28, a gloss apparently, further emphasizes this central point.

This leaves the rest of v 4 (aside from v 4bβ¹)) and the unit vv 19-20 along with v 21 to be accounted for in the "Moses and they" narrative. Since v 5 has its commentary in vv 22 ff, in a sequence stressing obedience and disobedience respectively, we might expect some such similar commentary on v 4. As previously noted, vv 19-20 tell of the disobedience of the people. Now a well structured piece narrating the obedience of the people can be easily extracted from vv 16-18 by leaving aside vv 16b-17a.²) This piece would consist of vv 16aβ, 17b-18. Its structure is as follows: A B 1 2 3 /1' 2' 3' B' A':

v 16aβ:	A	liqᵉṭû
	B	ʾîš lᵉpî ʾoklô
	1	ʿomer
v 17b:	2	hammarbbe
	3	hammamʿiṭ
v 18:	1'	baʿomer
	2'	hammarbbe
	3'	hammamʿit
	B'	ʾiš lᵉpî ʾoklô
	A'	laqaṭû

The contents of this piece point up the obedience of the people in gathering the manna. It is counterbalanced by vv 19-20, which tell of the people's disobedience. Both together form a sort of commentary on v 4.

If the foregoing literary analysis is correct (with vv 16aβ, 17b-18 belonging here), the "Moses and they" narrative would consist of vv 4abα, 5, 16aβ, 17b-20, 22-27, 29-30. Verses 4bβ and 28 are excluded as additions of a similar type (cf. *torah* in both), while v 21 is still unaccounted for. Since the "Moses and they" narrative is embedded

---

¹) Verse 4bβ, a gloss akin to v 28, likewise focuses attention on the question of obedience. Both these verses are generally ascribed to D(tr) because of motif and style; cf Dt. 8, 2-5; 29, 4f. Whether they are pre-D(tr) or not does not faze our argument; cf. C. Brekelmans, "Die sogenannten deuteronomistischen Elemente in Genesis bis Numeri: ein Beitrag zur Vorgeschichte des Deuteronomiums," *Volume du Congrès: Genève* 1965 (Supplements to Vetus Testamentum XV; Leiden, 1966), 90-96. Our point is that stylistically and linguistically, they do not fit our context; but their motif does.

²) Verse 16aα can be conveniently set aside as an editorial addition deriving from the redactor responsible for interweaving the four narratives (the same words are repeated in v 32aα) or might be considered as linking what follows with v 4.

in the "Moses and the children of Israel" narrative, we would ascribe
v 21 to this latter narrative. Another reason for doing so is that v 21
has nothing in common with the interests of the remaining two narratives previously signalled out (cf. below).

As a result of the foregoing analysis and by process of exclusion,
the second narrative, that of "Moses and the children of Israel",
would consist of the following: vv 3ab, 11-15, 16b-17a, 21, 31 and
35a. Verse 3ab is neatly linked with vv 13 ff by vv 11-12, which serve
as a sort of relay station, stylistically passing along the movement of
the narrative while changing one set of key words for another:

v 3ab:	A		baśar	
	B		leḥem	
v 12:	a	A′	bên ha'arbbaîm baśar	
	b	B′	babboqer	leḥem
v 13:	a′		ba'ereb	
	b′		babboqer	

Verses 14 ff (i.e. the verses pertaining to this narrative) go on telling
about the children of Israel and the manna, with no backward glance
to what was previously said; this section is a straightforward narrative
with no special stylistic pretensions. This seems all the more surprising since vv 11-12 are a typical proof-oracle (the term is Zimmerli's
"Erweiswort" [1]), albeit in a form adapted to suit the context. Further,
although we might expect reference to the fulfillment of the oracle
further on in the narrative, such reference is not forthcoming.

Further consideration of this proof-oracle seems in order here,
for it might shed some light on the puzzling doublet in vv 7 and 8.
In its classical and older form, the pattern of such a proof-oracle runs
as follows, the text being 1 K 20,13: [2]

ko 'amar YHWH	prophetic formula
hara'îta 'et kol hehamôn haggadôl hazze	motivation
hinn^enî not^enô b^eyad^eka hayyôm	salvation message
w^eyada'ta ki 'ani YHWH	proof formula

---

[1] Cf. W. Zimmerli, "Das Wort des göttlichen Selbsterweises (Erweiswort):
eine prophetische Gattung," *Mélanges bibliques rédigés en l'honneur de A. Robert*
(Travaux de l'Institut catholique de Paris 4; n.p., 1957), 154-164.

[2] The example is taken from L. Alonso-Schökel, *Genera litteraria: annotationes
in usum alumnorum* (mimeographed; Rome, 1965) 22 of the section "Gen. litt.
proph."

The formal feature of this pattern that distinguishes it from other prophetic and message patterns is the distinctive formula: "and you shall know that I am YHWH," deriving from prophetic preaching or judicial practice. Along with this, the salvation message usually has the formula, "natan b^eyad," which derives from the holy war formulary.[1]

The proof-oracle pattern derives from the messenger method of communication common to the oral culture of the early Semitic world. A good example of this method is the commissioning of a messenger as found in Gen 32, 4-6:[2]

wayyišlaḥ ya'qob mal'akim l^epanaw		notice of mission
'el 'eśaw 'aḥiw	to whom	address
'arṣa ś^e'ir śede 'edom	where	
wayyeṣaw 'otam le'mor		commission of message
ko to'merûn la'doni 1^e'eśaw		
ko 'amar 'abd^eda ya'qob		message formula
'im laban garti wa'eḥar 'ad 'atta		narration
wayy^ehî lî ṣôr waḥmôr w^eṣo'n		
w^e'ebed w^ešipḥa		
wa'ešl^eḥa l^ehaggîd la'doni limṣo'		intention
ḥen b^e'êneka		

Now the pattern evidenced in our passage (Ex 16, 11-12) is as follows:

wayy^edabber YHWH 'el-Moše le'mor	dialogue indicator
šama'tî 'et-t^elûnnot b^enê yiśra'el	motivation
dabber '^alehem le'mor	commission of message
bên ha'arbbaîm to'k^elû baśar	salvation message (narration?)
ûbabboqer tiśb^e'û-leḥem	
wiyda'tem kî '^anî YHWH '^elohêkem	proof formula

A comparison of this pattern with the aforementioned ones easily points up the composite character of the pattern in our verses, possibly due to adaptation to the context. In the first place, what makes vv 11-12 unlike the proof-oracle are the absence of the prophetic formula as well as the "natan b^eyad" formula, plus the intrusion of the formula for the commissioning of a message. Because of the pre-

---

[1] *Ibid.*
[2] This example is also taken from Alonso-Schökel, *op. cit.*, 5 of the section "Gen. litt. proph."

sence of this latter formula, the following message might be taken either as a salvation message or simply a narration of fact. After all, vv 11-12 do have the commission of a message and narration in common with the pattern cited above from Gen 32, 4-6. On the other hand, the distinctive "and you shall know that I am YHWH your God" does seem to indicate that the pattern is meant to be a proof-oracle.[1]) This is further borne out by the presence of the same pattern in Ex 6, 2-8 in a much more expanded form:

v 2: wayyᵉdabber ʾelohîm ʾel-Moše	dialogue indicator
wayyomer ʾelaw ʾanî YHWH . . .	
v 5: wᵉgam ʾanî šamaʿtî ʾet-naʾaqat	motivation
bᵉnê yiśraʾel	
v 6: laken ʾemor libᵉnê yiśraʾel	commission of message
ʾanî YHWH wᵉhoṣeʾtî ʾetᵉkem. . .	salvation message
v 7: wᵉlaqaḥtî ʾetᵉkem. . .	
wiydaʿ tem kî ʾanî YHWH ʾelohêkem	proof formula

The contents of this passage leave no doubt regarding the fact that it is meant to be a proof-oracle. Verse 9 tells of Moses' delivering the message to the people, an item lacking in our passage, as well as of the people's refusal to accept it.

Now since the passage concerning us here (Ex 16, 11-12) has the motivation, salvation message and proof formula features of the proof-oracle pattern, and is identical in pattern with Ex 6, 2-8 which is definitely a proof-oracle, it follows that our passage is likewise a proof-oracle.

This now leads to the problem of the doublet in vv 6-7 and 8 of the "Moses, Aaron and the whole congregation of the children of Israel" narrative. A cursory reading of these verses shows the similarity as well as the slight difference in the passage. Both pieces evidence an identical pattern:

v 6: wayyoʾmer Moše wᵉʾAharon . . .	dialogue indicator
ʿereb wiydaʿtem kî YHWH hôṣîʾ	proof (salvation message)
ʾetᵉkem	

---

[1]) The cultic prophet Ezechiel has made large use of this formula with proof-oracles adapted and amplified to meet his needs, so much so that the formula is characteristic of him; cf. Ez. 6, 7.13; 7, 4.9; 11, 10.12; 12, 20; 13, 9.14; 14,8; 15, 7; 17, 21; 20, 38.42.44; 22, 22; 23, 49; 24, 24; 25, 5; 35, 9; 36, 11; 37, 6.13.14; cf. also W.Zimmerli, *Erkenntnis Gottes nach dem Buch Ezechiel: eine theologische Studie* (Abhandlungen zur Theologie des Alten und Neuen Testaments 27; Zurich, 1954).

v 7: ûboqer ûre'îtem 'et-kebôd YHWH
    bišemô' YHWH 'et-telunnotêkem   motivation (for YHWH)
    wenaḥnû . . .   parenthesis
v 8: wayyo'mer Moše   dialogue indicator
    betet YHWH lakem ba'ereb baśar . . . proof (salvation message)
    weleḥem babboqer . . .
    bišemo' YHWH 'et-telunnotêkem   motivation (for YHWH)
    wenaḥnû . . .   parenthesis

Obviously both pieces inform the people (here: the whole congregation of the children of Israel) of the contents of the proof-oracle in vv 11-12. We would naturally have expected them after this oracle, as indicated by the parallel quoted above from Ex 6, 2-8. Further, the presence of the verb "natan" at the outset of v 8 suggests the classical proof-oracle, as does the "wiyda'tem kî YHWH" of v 7. These links with vv 11-12 naturally suggest the problem: do either or both of these passages belong after vv 11-12. Perhaps the dialogue indicators offer a key to some solution. In the first of the doublets, the speakers are Moses and Aaron, while in the second, Moses alone. Hence perhaps v 8 belongs someplace within the "Moses and they" narrative, possibly as the fulfillment of the command given Moses in v 12aβ (commission of message). On the other hand, v 8 is an incomplete sentence. Verse 8a seems to have been lifted bodily from a proof-oracle (salvation message), while v 8b is an almost verbatim citation of v 7aβb. If these are citations and voluntary dislocations effected by the redactor responsible for fusing the four narratives, they may have been placed in v 8 to link the "Moses, Aaron, whole congregation" narrative with what follows, namely the desert feeding.[1] The problem seems insoluble. We shall consider v 8 as the work of a redactor whose aim was to relate the "Moses, Aaron, whole congregation" narrative to the overall context of Ex 16.

Verse 35 appears to be the fusion of the conclusions to the "Moses and the children of Israel" narrative and the "Moses and they" narrative. The intervention of the words "forty years" mars the structure of the conclusion. Its present pattern runs A B C 1/B' A' 1':

A   'akelû
B   'et-hamman
C   'arbba'îm šana

---

[1] This is Coppens' position (with Kuenen), *art. cit.*, 477.

1	'ad-bo'am
B'	'et-hamman
A'	'ak^elû
1'	'ad-bo'am

Hence the mention of "forty years" seems to be an addition. Its obvious purpose is to indicate that the "children of Israel" did not come to inhabited land until forty years had passed. The addition thus closely links v 35a to v 35b ("to the border of the land of Canaan"), with the result that the whole of Ex 16 is closely tied to Josh 5, 10-12 (cf. below).

Finally, there is v 36, which seems to be a redactional gloss, since it does not tie in stylistically with any of the aforementioned narratives and offers an item of antiquarian interest.

Thus on the basis of the cast of characters in Ex 16 along with stylistic indications, there are four narratives [1] in the chapter, along with some additions or glosses. These would be:

1) Moses, Aaron and the whole congregation: vv 1-2, 3c, 6-7, 9-10.
2) Moses and the children of Israel: vv 3ab, 11-15, 16b-17a, 21, 31, 35a.
3) Moses and they: vv 4abα, 5, 16a, 17b, 18-20, 22-27, 28-30, 35b.
4) Moses and Aaron: vv 32-34.

The additions or glosses: vv 4bβ, 8, 16aα, 28, 36.

Here then are the texts of the four narratives in synoptic fashion, with the glosses or additions in italics:

| 1 | 3 | 2 |

1. Then they set out from Elim and all the congregation of the children of Israel came to the desert of Sin, which is between Elim and Sinai, *on the* 15*th day of the second month since their departing from the land of Egypt.* [2]

---

[1] Coppens, *art. cit.*, 476, speaks of three narratives, a certain number of ligatures and glosses. But why vv 32-34 should be only an editorial gloss and not a narrative is not clear, since any of the narratives might be a gloss to the other.

[2] For the reason why we consider this dating a gloss, cf. 18 f. below.

1	3	2

2. Then then the whole con-
gation of the children of Israel
murmured against Moses and
against Aaron in the desert.

3ab. And the children of Israel
said to them (read: him): Would
that we had died by the hand of
YHWH in the land of Egypt,
when we sat by the meat pot,
when we ate bread to the full.

3c. For you have brought us
out to this desert to kill this
whole assembly with hunger.

4. Then YHWH said to Moses:
Behold I am going to rain bread for
you from heaven and the people will
go out and gather a day's portion
everyday, *so that I might test them,
whether they will walk in my Torah or
not.*

5. And on the 6th day, when they
prepare what they will have brought
in, it will be twice as much as they
can daily gather.

6. So Moses and Aaron said
to all (the congregation of) the
children of Israel: At evening you
shall know that YHWH brought
you out from the land of Egypt,

7. and in the morning you
shall see the glory of YHWH,
since he hears your murmurings
against YHWH; and what are we
that you murmur against us?

1   3   2

8. *Then Moses said: Since YHWH will give you meat to eat in the evening and bread to the full in the morning since YHWH hears your murmurings which you murmur against him; and what are we? Your murmurings are not against us but against YHWH.*

9. Then Moses said to Aaron: Say to the whole congregation of Israel: Draw near before YHWH, for he has heard your murmurings.

10. And while Aaron spoke to the whole congregation of the children of Israel, they turned facing the desert, and behold the glory of YHWH appeared in the cloud.

11. Then YHWH spoke to Moses saying:

12. I have heard the murmurings of the children of Israel. Speak to them saying: At twilight you shall eat flesh and in the morning you shall be filled with bread; then you shall know that I am YHWH your God.

13. In the evening quail came up and covered the camp, and in the morning there was a layer of dew around the camp.

14. Then the layer of dew went up, and behold on the surface of the desert there was something

1   3   2

fine, flake-like, fine like hoarfrost on the ground.

15. When the children of Israel saw, they said to one another: is it manna? for they did not know what it was. Then Moses said to them: This is the bread which YHWH has given you to eat.

16. *This is the thing that YHWH commands*: Gather of it, every man as much as he can eat, an omer apiece.

16b. You shall take according to the number of persons each has in his tent.

17a. And the children of Israel did so.

17b. They gathered, some more, some less.

18. Then they measured by the omer, and the one with more had nothing over, while the one with less had nothing lacking—they gathered, every man as much as he could eat.

19. Then Moses said to them: Let no man leave any of it ill morning.
20. But they did not listen to Moses. Some men left some of it over till morning, and it bred worms and stank. So Moses grew angry with them.

21. And they gathered it morning by morning, each one as

1   3   2

much as he could eat; but when the sun grew hot, it melted.

22. Then on the 6th day they gathered a double amount of bread, two omers each. Then all the men of the assembly came and told Moses.

23. Then he said to them: This is what YHWH says: Tomorrow is a day of solemn rest, a holy Sabbath to YHWH. What you will bake, bake! What you will boil, boil! And all that is left over, put it aside for yourselves to be kept till morning.

24. So they set it aside till the morning as Moses commanded. And it did not become rotten, and there was no worm in it.

25. Then Moses said: Eat today, for today is a Sabbath to YHWH. You shall not find it in the field today.

26. Six days you shall gather it, but on the 7th day, a Sabbath, there shall be none on it.

27. But on the 7th day some of the people went out to gather, but they did not find.

28. *Then YHWH said to Moses: How long do you refuse to keep my commandments and my Torah?*

29. See! Because YHWH has given you the Sabbath, therefore he gives you on the 6th day bread for two

4	3	2

days. Remain everyone at home. No one go out from his place on the 7th day.

30. So the people rested on the 7th day.

31. So the house (read: children) of Israel called its name "man." And it was white, like coriander seed, and its taste was was like honey cake.

32. Then Moses said: This is the thing that YHWH commands: A full omer of it is to be kept for your generations, so that they might see the bread with which I fed you in the desert upon my leading you out from the land of Egypt.

33. So Moses said to Aaron: Take one jar and put in it a full omer of manna, and place it before YHWH to be kept for your generations.

34. As YHWH commanded Moses, so did Aaron place it before the testimony to be kept.

35a. And the children of Israel ate the manna *40 years* till they came to inhabited land.

35b. They ate the manna till they came to the border of the land of Canaan.

36. *An omer is a tenth of an epha.*

Now what do these narratives have to say about the manna?

1) The "Moses, Aaron and the whole congregation" narrative has nothing to say about the manna. Rather, this account presents us with the sight of Israel trodding through the wilderness in liturgical procession ('adat, qahal). The assembly complains about hunger and is rewarded by turning toward the desert to find YHWH in theophany.[1]) Thus the narrative inculcates the same lesson in action as Dt 8,3 does in words. Perhaps it also insinuates the ideal of returning to the desert to find YHWH. The word "desert" is a key word in the narrative (vv 1, 2, 3c, 10), and the negative "murmuring in the desert" theme is balanced and perhaps outweighed by the positive "theophany in the desert" theme.[2])

2) The "Moses and the children of Israel" narrative, on the other hand, treats entirely about the manna. Israel's complaints about food are here rewarded with a proof-oracle to Moses promising salvation, here meat and bread. After the single mention of quail here (v 13), the narrative continues focused solely upon the manna. It is possible that no further mention of quail is made because the recorder(s) of this tradition wished to treat of the manna alone. On the other hand it is equally possible that they were aware of the tradition of the calamity associated with the quail (cf. Nb 11). This latter alternative is intimated by the fact that the quail come in the evening, the manna in the morning. For in the Bible, the morning is generally the period when God's saving help is experienced, while the evening and night are times of punishment.[3])

The description of the manna given here is prosaic, a description of fact with nothing miraculous about it. And the narrative itself does not seem to make any theological point. What is underlined is the origin of the word "*man*" (cf. the pun in v 15 and v 31). The only

---

[1]) This narrative is an example of P's *kabod* theology according to G. von Rad, *Studies in Deuteronomy* (Studies in Biblical Theology 9; London, 1953), 41 ff. Von Rad writes (41-42): "The question of the provenance of P resolves itself, in our opinion, fundamentally into the question of the provenance of this Kabod-Moed theology which is dominant in it. One immediately thinks of Ezekiel." As pointed out above (8, n. 1), the proof pattern in the "Moses and the children of Israel" narrative likewise recalls Ezekiel.

[2]) The presence of a positive or negative attitude toward Israel's desert period cannot be used to date or catalogue a given text; C. Barth, "Zur Bedeutung der Wüstentradition," *Volume du Congrès: Genève* 1965 (Supplements to Vetus Testamentum XV; Leiden, 1966), 14-23, shows that both attitudes are in evidence throughout the biblical period.

[3]) Cf. J. Ziegler, "Die Hilfe Gottes 'am Morgen'," *Alttestamentliche Studien Friedrich Nötscher... gewidmet* (Bonner biblische Beiträge I; Bonn, 1950), 281-288.

hint the narrative offers about the manna as a miraculous food is the statement in v 35a taken with the gloss [1]) that Israel ate the manna for forty years, thus presupposing a continuous supply. Without the gloss, v 35a concludes the narrative with the statement: "And the children of Israel ate the manna till they came to inhabited land." Now this inhabited land need not necessarily mean Canaan, as the present context of this narrative connotes. Rather it could and probably does mean a settlement situated a few day's march from the Israelite encampment.[2])

3) The "Moses and they" narrative is a clear example of halakic midrash,[3]) in which the author uses the manna tradition as a springboard for inculcating obedience to the Sabbath precept. For example, v 26 is a clear paraphrase and adaptation of a piece of legislation like Ex 31,15 or Lev 23, 3, [4]) while v 23 seems to be a homiletic application of a part of the manna narrative of Nb 11, 6-9. In the "Moses and they" narrative, the manna is clearly miraculous, a veritable Pavlovian object lesson on the Sabbath rest: "Because YHWH has given you the Sabbath, therefore he gives you on the 6th day bread for two days" (v 29). The manna is doled out in miraculous amounts, YHWH taking care that all get enough. Verse 35b concludes the midrash as well as the chapter; it tells that YHWH took care to feed his people miraculously right till their entry into Canaan thus preparing for the account of the final feeding in Josh 5, 10-12.

4) The "Moses and Aaron" narrative is of a clearly Priestly stamp.[5]) What its purpose is here [6]) in Ex 16 is hard to say, considering that P

---

[1]) Cf. 9-10 above; on the number "forty," cf. J. Gray, "The Desert Sojourn of the Hebrews and the Sinai-Horeb Tradition," *VT* 4 (1954), 153-154 and the observation by H. J. Kraus, *Worship in Israel*, trans. G. Buswell (Oxford, 1966), 41, that numbers in the ancient Near East are often to be assessed qualitatively and not quantitatively.

[2]) Cf. W. Beyerlin, *Origins and History of the Oldest Sinaitic Traditions*, trans. S. Rudman (Oxford, 1965), 146, n. 7: "It is quite misleading to think of the Israelites wandering aimlessly for forty years in the desert. As ass-using nomads these groups could never have been more than a short day's march from water." Nor could they have been very far from food either.

[3]) Cf. R. Bloch, "Midrash," *DBS*, V, cols. 1263-1281, and for examples of other midrashim in the O.T., cf. especially col. 1271 ff.; *idem*, "Ezéchiel XVI: exemple parfait du procédé midrashique dans la Bible," *Cahiers Sioniens* 9 (1955), 193-223; S. Sandmel, "The Haggada within Scripture," *JBL* 80 (1961), 105-122; A. G. Wright, "The Literary Genre Midrash," *CBQ* 28 (1966), 105-138; 417-457.

[4]) Cf. p. 29 f. below.

[5]) Cazelles, *art. cit.*, col. 847 assigns it to Ps, a Priestly supplement.

[6]) The purpose of the narrative in itself is clear—the jar of manna will bear

narrates the institution of the Testimony only in Ex 24, 16. This latter passage also tells of the descent of the glory of YHWH in the form of a cloud. Perhaps this "Moses and Aaron" narrative was part of the tradition contained in our "Moses, Aaron and the whole congregation" narrative and crept into this chapter with that narrative. Be that as it may, it does tell us again of a miraculous manna which remains not just overnight or over the Sabbath eve, but for generations.

b) *The Unity of Ex* 16

While it is quite apparent that Ex 16 consists of several narratives, each with its own interests and agents, it is no less apparent that the chapter forms a well knit unity. However the unity does not derive from theme or style of composition, but from chronology. This item has been pointed out by P. Skehan in his review of A. Jaubert's significant work, *La Date de la Cène* (EB Paris 1957).[1] Jaubert has adequately proved [2] that the calendar of the book of Jubilees was used by the P tradition redactors in their work on the Hexateuch, as well as in Chronicles, Ezra-Nehemia, and Ezechiel.[3] In these texts the dates of events are expressed in numbers, in the manner of the calendar of the book of Jubilees.

---

continual witness to YHWH's goodness and concern as revealed to the wilderness generation in the miraculous feeding; cf. Te Stroete, *Exodus*, 123.

[1] P. Skehan, "The Date of the Last Supper," *CBQ* 20 (1958), 194-195.

[2] Cf. Jaubert, *La Date de la Cène*, 31-41. The only strong criticism against Jaubert's thesis has come from E. Kutsch, "Der Kalender des Jubiläenbuches und das Alte und das Neue Testament," *VT* 11 (1961), 39-47; but H. Cazelles, "Sur les origines du calendrier des Jubilés," *Biblica* 43 (1962), 202-212, and (E. Vogt), "Note sur le calendrier du Déluge," *Biblica* 43 (1962), 212-216, have rejected most of Kutsch's views as untenable. Cf. also E. Ruckstuhl, *Chronology of the Last Days of Jesus*, trans. V. Drapela (New York, 1965), 72 ff.

[3] This calendar, as reconstructed by Jaubert, *op. cit.*, 26, is as follows; the days and months are unnamed and fixed, the liturgical days being the 1st, 4th and 6th days:

Month	I, IV, VII, X					II, V, VIII, XI					III, VI, IX, XII				
4th day	1	8	15	22	29		6	13	20	27		4	11	18	25
5th day	2	9	16	23	30		7	14	21	28		5	12	19	26
6th day	3	10	17	24		1	8	15	22	29		6	13	20	27
Sabbath	4	11	18	25		2	9	16	23	30		7	14	21	28
1st day	5	12	19	26		3	10	17	24		1	8	15	22	29
2nd day	6	13	20	27		4	11	18	25		2	9	16	23	30
3rd day	7	14	21	28		5	12	19	26		3	10	17	24	31

Now as Skehan has indicated, Ex 16 covers the course of one week:

v 1: the liturgical procession arrives on the 15th day of the second month = Friday, i.e. in time to observe the Sabbath rest. The people murmur; they are promised food (vv 2-5), as well as (or perhaps especially) the vision of the glory of YHWH, which will come "in the evening" and "in the morning," i.e. last for the whole Sabbath.

vv 9-13: Sabbath — a theophany takes place; Moses is given a proof-oracle to the effect that when the Sabbath is over ("at twilight") the people shall have meat, and on the following morning (Sunday), bread.

v 13a: at the end of the Sabbath, "in the evening," the quail come and

vv 13b-20: "in the morning," the first day of the manna, the people find it and gather it.

v 21: the people gather it every morning (hypothetically, from Monday to Thursday, i.e. every morning of this week).

vv 22-24: on the 6th day, they receive a double amount, i.e. on Friday.

vv 25-30: the Sabbath rest.

Obviously, the interests of the redactor responsible for the unity of this chapter are chronological. Certainly the indication of time in v 1 derives from him. And perhaps the "Moses and they" narrative, the halakic midrash, derives from the same source, as does the "forty years" notation in v 35.

Within the chronological framework of the chapter as it now stands, the manna comes out second best as a focus of interest. What the redactor now emphasizes is the Sabbath theophany and the Sabbath rest. Just as in the "Moses and they" narrative, the manna is an object lesson, inculcating the Sabbath precept. The "Moses and Aaron" narrative becomes a gloss.

In conclusion, then, Ex 16 consists of four narratives, three of which are unified chronologically by a Priestly redactor to bring home the lesson of the Sabbath observance, the fourth inserted as a gloss. Of the four narratives, three are clearly the result of Priestly concern: the "Moses, Aaron and the whole congregation" narrative (1); the "Moses and they" narrative (3); and the "Moses and Aaron" narrative (4). Of these three, the last two highlight the miraculous nature of the manna. On the other hand, the "Moses and the children of Israel" narrative (2) presents a straightforward account of Israel's once having eaten manna in the wilderness. However the mention of the quail along with the proof-oracle of vv 11-12 suggest that this narrative is composite. Perhaps, as Noth has suggested though not in regard to our verses,[1]) the sober account of the feeding of Israel originally belonged to Nb 11, where J treats of this theme. Perhaps also, the P redactor(s) saw fit to put it here for reasons of literary balance. For the Pentateuch narrative persents the tradition of the quail, the manna and the well both before and after the great Sinai theophany.[2]) And P sees fit to do the same with the inculcation of the Sabbath precept, which seems to be the whole point of Ex 16 as it now stands.[3]) Or, finally, it may be P's way of further pointing out in significant fashion that the unique God of creation (Gen 1 = P) is the same God responsible for the new creation of the Exodus and its results; God's Sabbath rest in Ex 16 together with the week-chronology clearly link both chapters, i.e. Gen 1 and Ex 16.

2) *Nb* 11, 6-9

The Exodus event and the Sinai event are parallel in several respects. One of these is the fact that almost immediately after both events, the Pentateuch narrative tells of the complaint of the people about food, their longing after Egypt, and finally a providential feeding of the people. Ex 16 tells of the post-Exodus feeding, while Nb 11 narrates the post-Sinai feeding, though it highlights the coming of the quail and not the manna.[4]) The manna is mentioned here only in vv 6b-9, in almost parenthetical fashion.

---

[1]) M. Noth, *Überlieferungsgeschichte des Pentateuch* (Stuttgart, 1948), 32, n. 110; on the same page, Noth regards only vv 4ab, 5, 29-31, 35b, 36 as belonging to J. Hence "presumably the oldest Old Testament passage about the sabbath" derives from J here, as Noth notes in his *Exodus: A Commentary*, trans. J. S. Bowden (Old Testament Library; London, 1962), 136.

[2]) Cf. O. Eissfeldt, *Hexateuch-Synopse* (2d ed.; Darmstadt, 1962), 41 f.

[3]) Cf. G. Auzou, *De la servitude au service* (Paris, 1961), 226.

[4]) Nb 11 has not a few traits in common with Ex 16: chronologically, the discussion in Nb 11, 1-23 takes place on Friday (at the end of three days journey—Nb 10, 33—begun on the 20th day of the 2nd month, which according to the Jubilees' calendar is a Wednesday—Nb 10, 11); the people are to consecrate themselves for the next day, Sabbath (Nb 11, 18). The theophany (Nb 11, 24-25) apparently, and the quail certainly, come on the Sabbath. But unlike Ex 16, here the people go to gather the quail on the Sabbath itself (Nb 11, 31). Hence along with the other motives provoking divine punishment in Nb 11, we might also enumerate the insinuated non-observance of the Sabbath.

Modern critics are quite agreed that this account of the manna is certainly not P. Gray [1]) calls it a JE account; Eissfeldt [2]) sees v 6 as belonging to the J tradition, while vv 7-9 belong to E; Cazelles [3]) considers the whole passage (i.e. vv 6-9) as E's account of the manna; while Noth [4]) deems vv 6aβb-9 as J, Nb 11 being the original locus of J's manna account, now displaced and colored over by P in Ex 16.

Noth [5]) is certainly correct in calling this passage a "foreign body" in Nb 11, for vv 6aβb-9 can be conveniently omitted without affecting the flow of the narrative at all. Perhaps the passage was retained, or better, replaced here in its present clumsy form with a view to harmonizing the narrative of the people's complaint with the previous Pentateuch mention of a continuous manna supply. Be that as it may, the passage before us consists of a restrictive clause casually mentioning the manna in the complaint of the people, followed by a parenthetic account describing the manna and the modes of preparing it.

(6aα: But now our soul is dried up)
v 6aβb: there is nothing at all except our eyes upon the manna.
vv 7-9: Now the manna was like coriander seed, and its appearance like the appearance of bdellium. The people went about and gathered and ground in mills or crushed in a mortar and boiled in a pot and made it into cakes. And its taste was like the taste of oil cake. When the dew came down upon the camp at night, the manna came down upon it.

Among the new items of information about the manna contributed by this passage, we find that the manna is like bdellium. Further, it has the qualities of grain, since it can be ground in mills or crushed in a mortar, information omitted in the Exodus account (16,23). And since it was like grain, it could be made into cakes.[6])

---

[1]) G. B. Gray, *A Critical and Exegetical Commentary on Numbers* (ICC; Edinburgh, 1903), 100-101.
[2]) Eissfeldt, *Hexateuch-Synopse*, 161*.
[3]) Cazelles, *DBS*, VII, col. 806; cf. col. 789.
[4]) Noth, *Überlieferungsgeschichte des Pentateuch*, 34, n. 119.
[5]) *Ibid.*; cf. also Gray, *loc. cit.* and 105-106.
[6]) This further information in the Nb account of the manna seems much like a haggadic expansion of the manna tradition. The mills and mortar suggest reference to a sedentary people used to working with grain, not to desert nomads. Such expansion in later (and earlier) tradition is not surprising, considering that the complaints about food raised by the Israelites in the desert are in no way considered to contradict the information of Ex 12, 37-38 that they had their flocks along with themselves.

The Exodus description of the manna and the Nb account either belong to two different traditions or are amplifications of the same tradition. This point is borne out, first of all, by the information about the taste of the manna. Ex 16, 31 tells us that the manna tasted like honey cake, while Nb 11,8 says it tasted like oil cake. Further, Nb 11,9 informs us that when the night dew descended upon the camp, the manna came down upon it, with no further specific mention of when the manna came down, hence presumably at night. Ex 16, 13-14 tells of the manna being found when the layer of dew evaporated in the morning, with no further specific mention of when the dew was formed. These descriptions of the dew formation may be variant reports of the same phenomenon; however, there is one important difference. Ex 16, 13-14 gives no intimation that the manna *came down* at all; this is a deduction from v 4. As a matter of fact, taken within the context of the "Moses and the children of Israel" narrative, vv 13-14 imply that the manna was simply there on the ground, formed there overnight. The only point of contact between the "Moses and the children of Israel" narrative and Nb 11, 6-9 is the mention in both that the manna was like coriander seed. On the other hand, Nb 11, 6-9 does agree with the midrashic "Moses and they" narrative on the point that the manna descends from above.

However, the fact that the Nb account speaks of manna as "coming down" need not imply anything miraculous; it may be a phenomenological interpretation of the same happening described in Ex 16, 13-14. Yet the manner in which the Nb description is related in its present context does presuppose the manna to be something miraculous. For by linking the mention of the manna with the complaint in vv 4-6aα, the redactor of this chapter of Nb implies that the Israelites always had a continuous supply of manna to meet their daily needs.

3) *Nb* 21,5

Nb 21, 4-9 narrates the history of the origin of the bronze snake, revered in the Jerusalem temple to about 700 B.C. [1] The critics set aside v 4a as deriving from P, while they differ as to what layer of the Pentateuchal traditions the rest of the narrative belongs. Gray [2]

---

[1] Cf. O. Eissfeldt, *The Old Testament: An Introduction*, trans. P. Ackroyd (London, 1965), 44.

[2] Gray, *Numbers* (ICC), 277.

assigns it to JE; Eissfeldt [1]), to E; while Noth, [2]) after a long and specialized study of this chapter, concludes that the source of our passage is dubious at least, and that it is a secondary element in the chapter as it now stands.

The passage tells of the people's renewed complaint against Moses and God over lack of food and water:

v 5: Then the people spoke against God and against Moses: Why have you brought us up from Egypt to die in the desert, for there is no bread and there is no water, and we loathe this worthless bread.

It was this complaint that provoked God to send the fiery serpents among the people.

The "worthless [3]) bread" mentioned here is undoubtedly the manna of the previous Pentateuch accounts. Coppens [4]) notes in passing that this text seems to be ignorant of the fact that YHWH granted his people a special miraculous nourishment in the course of its desert wanderings, because the passage implies that the nourishment of the people in the desert was meager and mediocre. On the other hand, this may be precisely what the author of this aetiological account of the snake wants to imply as being the attitude of the people, that the manna was meager and mediocre in their eyes. He would thus underline the wickedness of the desert generation as well as the justice of the punishment that follows.[5])

Yet the complaint may reflect a tradition according to which the manna provided the children of Israel was really meager and mediocre nourishment. In this perspective, the following punishment may be interpreted as due to Israel's lack of gratitude for whatever good things YHWH had provided them with during their desert wanderings, regardless of how meager and mediocre those things might appear to later generations.

---

[1]) Eissfeldt, *Hexateuch-Synopse*, 180*-181*.

[2]) M. Noth, "Num. 21 als Glied der 'Hexateuch'-Erzählung," *ZAW* 58 (1940/41), 180, and for v 5 especially 178. Cf. also his *Überlieferungsgeschichte des Pentateuch*, 34, n. 123.

[3]) Literally: light. Cf. Gray, *Numbers* (ICC), 277: "*qᵉloqel* occurs only here, but the root in Heb. means literally *to be light*, and so *contemptible* (e.g. 2 S 19, 44 (43); Is 8, 23 (9,1)). On account of a *special* development of the root-meaning in Assyr. (*kalkaltu* = hunger), some interpret *qᵉloqel* here *unsatisfying*."

[4]) Coppens, *art. cit.*, 474.

[5]) We shall see below that this is precisely how the Palestinian exegesis in the Targums understood the complaint.

Before considering Dt 8, it would be useful to consider the points of similarity in the foregoing Pentateuchal mentions of the manna:

(a) The manna references are intimately bound up with Israel's complaint about food in the desert.

(b) This manna—food complaint motif is rooted in a longing to return to Egypt, hence it entails a rejection of the liberation wrought by YHWH.

(c) The complaint about food and/or manna directed against Moses is consistently interpreted as being really against YHWH, hence a "tempting" or a rejection of YHWH.[1]

(d) The *giving* of the manna is never interpreted directly in haggadic fashion, as having a deeper theological significance, though the foregoing narratives evidence haggadic interpretations of the manna itself. Rather the manna event is used as an object lesson in a halakic midrash inculcating the Sabbath rest (Ex 16) or to punctuate the food complaint motif (Nb).

4) *Dt* 8, 3.16

Dt 8, 1-18 is a parenetic sermon aimed at instilling obedience to the commandments of YHWH as set forth by Moses on Deuteronomy's "this day" (v 11). That is the central point of the chiastic structure of this passage, in which the verses on the manna (vv 3, 16) rank as corresponding members. [2] These statements on the manna are novel:

v 3: And he humbled you and made you hunger and fed you the manna which you did not know and which your fathers did not know, so that he might make you know that not on bread alone does man live, but on everything proceeding from YHWH's mouth does man live.

v 16: (he who) was feeding you manna in the desert which your fathers did not know so that he might humble you and so that he might test you to do you good in the end.

Here for the first time in the Pentateuch transmission of the manna motif, the giving of the manna undergoes a haggadic, "spiritual"

---

[1] Cf. H. Kruse, "Die 'dialektische Negation' als semitisches Idiom," *VT* 4 (1951), 389-390.

[2] Cf. N. Lohfink, *Das Hauptgebot: eine Untersuchung literarischer Einleitungsfragen zu Dtn* 5-11 (Analecta Biblica 20; Rome, 1963), 189-199, especially 194-195 and 292.

interpretation.[1]) It is not merely an object less for some halaka, as in Ex 16, but is itself the vehicle of a deeper truth. Thus with the Dtr handling of the matter, the desert nourishment of the manna takes on midrashic traits of a haggadic nature.[2]) Von Rad [3]) has well described the shift in emphasis:

> "Oddly enough, the priestly version of the story of the manna [4]) approximates after a fashion to this version of it [5]) — all gathered the manna which came down; but it turned out in the evening that everyone had gathered the exact quantity necessary for himself and his family — there was no surplus and no lack. One meaning of what happened became clear here. The event comes to have typological significance — God gives to each according to his need. And further, the manna cannot be stored up. A few did try to do so, but they found that it went bad (Ex 16, 9-27). In this case too, history is intended to be the dress for a truth which Israel arrived at from her relations with Jahweh — this daily sustenance by God demanded a surrender without security: in dealing with God, we live from minute to minute. In the story of the manna as Deuteronomy understood

---

[1]) Cf. Eissfeldt, *Hexateuch-Synopse*, 41: "Geistliche Ausdeutung älterer realistisch gemeinter Erzählungen findet sich nicht nur in den Apokryphen und Pseudo-epigraphen und im Neuen Testament, sondern auch im Alten Testament selbst. Im Deuteronomium wird die Manna-Erzählung geistlich ausgedeutet..."

[2]) Cf. S. R. Driver, *A Critical and Exegetical Commentary on Deuteronomy* (ICC; Edinburgh, 1902), 106-107: "In particular the manna is pointed to, as illustrating the discipline of the wilderness: Israel's self-sufficiency was 'humbled,' first by its being suffered to feel a want, and afterwards by the manner in which its want was supplied; it was thus taught how, for its very existence, it was daily (Ex. 16, 4) dependent on the (creative) word of God... Further, the manna 'proved' Israel (v 16: Ex 16, 4) by showing, viz. whether or not Israel would accommodate itself, trustfully and contentedly (Nu 21, 5) to this state of continued dependence upon God, and whether therefore it could be trusted to obey it. Thus the manna (1) taught Israel its dependence upon Jehovah, and (2) operated as a test of Israel's disposition... It was food unknown before (Ex. 16, 15); and consequently a signal evidence of God's sustaining providence. —That man doth not live on bread alone etc. the didactic treatment of the history continues, a further lesson being based upon the narrative of the manna. The narrative showed that the natural products of the earth are not uniformly sufficient for the support of life: the creative will of God, in whatever other way it may, upon occasion, specially exert itself, is also a sustaining power on which man may find himself obliged to rely."

[3]) G. von Rad, *Old Testament Theology*, trans. D. M. G. Stalker (New York, 1962), I, 282.

[4]) I.e. Ex. 16.

[5]) I.e. the view of the desert wanderings as the time when the relationship of YHWH and Israel was at its fairest, as depicted in Jer 2, 1-3. Such an interpretation of Jer 2, 1-3 has been subjected to careful criticism by C. Barth in his article on the meaning of the desert tradition, cited above 16, n. 2.

it, this process of spiritualizing the old miraculous story is carried a further step forward. In P, manna is after all food for the body, and nothing is yet explicitly said about the deeper meaning lying behind it, but in Deut. 8, 3, the matter is completely spiritualized. It is stated expressly that the event was intended to teach that man does not live by bread alone but 'by everything that proceeds from the mouth of Jahweh.' Here manna is obviously taken as spiritual food. In all this we have to bear in mind that the idea of a life in the wilderness became more and more incomprehensible to Israel after her settlement in the arable land and when she had come to enjoy the blessings of that land.''

Consequently, much like the preacher responsible for the "Moses and they" narrative in Ex 16, the preacher [1]) responsible for our present passage passes on the manna tradition while attempting to make it meaningful for his contemporaries.

5) *Josh* 5, 12

Josh 5, 10-12 is an easily discernible literary unit (cf. below). The text tells us:

v 10: While the children of Israel were encamped at Gilgal, they kept the Passover on the 14th day of the month in the evening on the plains of Jericho.
v 11: Then they ate of the produce of the land from the day after the Passover, unleavened bread and parched grain, on that very day.
v 12: Then the manna ceased from the day after, when they ate of the produce of the land. And the children of Israel no longer had manna, and they ate of the produce of the land of Canaan in that year.

The opinion of the critics on these verses is quite nuanced, based on rather varied reasons. Eissfeldt [2]) deems the passage to be an inde-

---

[1]) Cf. Von Rad, *Studies in Deuteronomy*, 11-24.
[2]) Eissfeldt, *Hexateuch-Synopse*, 69: ''(Josh) 5, 10-12 sind nach allgemeiner Anschauung P-Text. Indes hat schon Dillmann darauf hingewiesen, dass das Wort ᶜabur 'Ertrag' nur hier vorkommt, und Holzinger hat aus dieser Beobachtung und aus anderen die Folgerung gezogen, dass in v. 10-12 nicht glatter P-Text vorliege, dass vielmehr einiges daraus späterer Bearbeitung zuzuschreiben sei. Smend hat dann einen Anteil des P an v. 10-12 überhaupt bestritten. In der Tat ist die Zugehörigkeit des Stückes zu P ganz unwahrscheinlich. In Ex 16, 1-14 lässt P Manna und Wachteln zugleich gegeben werden. Wenn es sich da um eine wiederholte Spendung beider Gaben handelte, so müsste hier bei der Ankunft im Westjordanland neben dem Aufhören des Manna auch das Ende der Wachtelgabe von P erzählt sein. Aber wir sahen, dass Ex 16, 1-14 offenbar an eine ein-

pendent narrative because it cannot be P; it contradicts P's manna narrative (Ex 16, 1-14: manna and quail given together and only once). Noth [1]) likewise considers it independent; it cannot be P because of the singular phrase "unleavened bread and parched grain" (which are not found in P in this way) and because of the handling of the feasts mentioned with no reference to a divine precept. Only the time references are later additions. George [2]) too judges the passage as not P, but perhaps preserved in Priestly circles. Both Noth and George agree on the pre-Deuteronomistic character of the tradition in these verses, and with this Kraus [3]) agrees. Only Kraus considers the reference to the cessation of the manna in v 12 as an equally late addition. De Vaux [4]) also thinks our verses are an independent tradition, and with Kraus, deriving from Gilgal cult. Kutsch, [5])

---

malige Gabe von Manna und Wachteln gedacht ist. Dann widerspricht Jos 5, 10-12 der Manna-Erzählung des P und kann darum nicht P sein."

[1]) M. Noth, *Überlieferungsgeschichtliche Studien* (2d ed.; Tübingen, 1957), 183: "Dieses letztere Stück (i.e. Josh 5, 10-12) sitzt in der Tat recht lose im Zusammenhang der Landnahmegeschichten, aber auf P lässt es sich keinesfalls zurückführen; denn P (vgl. Ex. 12, 1 ff) hätte weder den völlig singulären Ausdruck 'Mazzen und Geröstetes' gebraucht, noch erst recht das Mazzenessen im Anschluss and das Passah statt auf ein göttliches Gebot vielmehr auf die Gelegenheit des für die israelitischen Stämme nach dem zeit frisch gereiften Getreides zurückgeführt. Nur sämtliche Zeitangaben in diesem Abschnitt sind nachträglich hinzugesetzt auf Grund der späteren datummässigen Festlegung des Passah-Mazzen Festes, wie sie erstmalig, wohl im Heiligkeitsgesetz (Lev. 23, 4 ff) begegnet." Cf. also his commentary, *Das Buch Josua* (Handbuch zum Alten Testament I/7, 2d ed.; Tübingen, 1953) on 5, 10-12.

[2]) A. George, "Les Récits de Gilgal en Josué (V, 2-15)," *Memorial J. Chaine* (Bibliothèque de la Faculté Catholique de Théologie de Lyon 5; Lyon, 1950), 175 ff.: "Littérairement celle-ci (i.e. Josh 5, 10-12) appartient à une autre source: son début nomme Gilgal comme si il n'en avait pas été question au verset précédent; le souci de chronologie précise... l'intérêt liturgique porté à la Pâque, aux azymes, l'allusion à la manne, l'expression caractéristique 'en l'os de ce jour'... sont autant d'indices que nos versets se rattachent à la littérature sacerdotale"; and n. 27, p. 175: "Noth (p. 17) a bien noté 'que l'on ne peut pas rattacher simplement ce fragment (v. 10-12) à P.' "

[3]) Kraus, *Worship in Israel*, 162: "We must begin, however, by separating two elements: the later dating in v. 10 ('on the fourteenth day of the month at even') and the reference in v. 12 to the cessation of the manna. Apart from these elements there are three important factors... It would be a hasty and hardly justifiable conclusion to take the whole passage vv. 10-12 out of its context and to take it to be a secondary construction in view of the later dating in v. 10" (against Kutsch; cf n. 5 below).

[4]) R. de Vaux, *Ancient Israel: Its Life and Institutions*, trans. J. McHugh (London, 1961), 488: "Rather the general impression is that Jos 5, 10-12 represents an independent tradition which reflects a custom of the sanctuary at Gilgal."

[5]) E. Kutsch, "Erwägungen zur Geschichte der Passafeier und des Massotfestes," *Zeitschrift für Theologie und Kirche* 55 (1958), 21: "Nun ist in V. 11 ausdrück-

on the other hand, provides a dissenting opinion; he holds the whole passage to be P because of the way the eating of the unleavened bread is tied in with the Passover. This trait is clearly post-Exilic and P.[1])

As with Ex 16, perhaps here too stylistic analysis can shed light on the purpose and provenance of the passage under consideration. As the text stands, [2]) the structure is as follows:

v 10:	1	children of Israel
	2	Gilgal (place)
	3	14th day of the (first) month in the evening (time)
v 11:	A	wayyo'kᵉlû me'ᵃbûr ha'areṣ
	B	mimmohᵒrat happesaḥ (not in LXX)

lich gesagt, dass das Massot-Essen am Tage nach dem Passa begann. M.a.W.: hier ist die terminliche Verbindung von Passafeier und Massotfest bereits vorausgesetzt. Daraus ergibt sich zwingend, dass diese Verse nicht eine Tradition aus der Richterzeit wiedergeben können. Man braucht auch nicht die Datumsangabe in V. 10 und die Worte 'an eben diesem Tage' in V. 11 allein als von einen priesterlichen Redaktion herrührend anzusehen. Der ganze Abschnitt Jos 5, 10-12 stammt vielmehr aus der Priesterschrift bzw. von einem naherstehenden Redaktor... Die Verbindung von Passafeier und Massotfest mit dem Lager in Gilgal gab dem priesterlichen Verfasser von Jos 5, 10-12 die Möglichkeit, das Ende des Mannasegens zu berichten und den mit dem Massot-Essen verbundenen Neuanfang zu unterstreichen, darüber hinaus aber auch noch den Jordandurchzug auf den 10, I zu datieren, der seinerseits in der Passaordnung bei P dadurch hervorgehoben ist, dass an ihm das Passatier ausgewählt werden soll."

[1]) *Ibid.*, 34: "Während vom Exil an (Ez. 45, 21-24; Lev. 23, 5-8, usw.) Passa (am Abend des 14.I.) und Massotfest (15.-21.I.) unmittelbar aufeinander folgten, wurden sie bis zum Exil unabhängig voneinander begangen..." Kutsch's position has been recently taken to task by J. Alberto Soggin, "Gilgal, Passah und Landnahme: eine neue Untersuchung des kultischen Zusammenhangs der Kap. III-VI des Josuabuches," *Volume du Congrès*: *Genève* 1965 (Supplements to Vetus Testamentum XV; Leiden, 1966), 273-274; Soggin insists that our passage contains an older tradition since even if post-Exilic, the text we have "schliesst aber nicht aus, dass eine ältere Tradition in einer späteren Epoche nach deren liturgischen, chronologischen und sonstigen Ansichten ausgebaut, bzw. aktualisiert werden konnte" (p. 273). Soggin's main argument is: "Wenn aber V, 10-12 eine viel spätere Überlieferung bilden, worauf zieht dann der ganze Abschnitt (i.e. Josh 3-4)?", since both the later chronological indications as well as the "Urfassung" focus upon the Passover related in our passage.

[2]) LXX lacks the three phrases indicated in the scheme above. If these were lacking in the LXX *Vorlage*, then the point emphasized in that *Vorlage* would be the change in food. However in this whole passage, the LXX goes its own targumizing way; cf. no mention of Gilgal; בערבות יריחו = ἐπὶ δυσμῶν Ἰεριχω ἐν τῷ πέραν τοῦ Ἰορδάνου ἐν τῷ πεδίῳ in v 10; קלוי = νέα in v 11; יאכלו = ἐκαρπίσαντο; and as always, כנען = φοινίκων in v 12.

	C	maṣṣot weqalûy (food)	
	D	be'eṣem hayyôm hazze	(not in LXX)
v 12:	C'	hamman (food)	
	B'	mimmoḥ°rat	(not in LXX)
	A'	be'oklam me'ᵃbûr ha'areṣ	
	1'	children of Israel	
	2'	land of Canaan (place)	
	3'	in that year (time)	

Both in style and contents, the passage before us is starkly reminiscent of Ex 16, and more specifically, of the "Moses and they"
narrative. There is the same interest in chronology, prescribed festal
time and food bound up with this festal time. The "till the land of
Canaan" and forty years mentioned in the "Moses and they" account
(v 35) are marked off here as ended. But the main point in the foregoing chiasm is "that very day," the day after the Passover when
the Israelites ate "unleavened bread and parched grain," thus obser-
ving the first feast of the Unleavened Bread at the precise time le-
gislated in the Holiness Code. As a matter of fact, the halakic midrash of Ex 16 on the Sabbath finds its counterpart here in the way
our passage focuses upon the feast of Unleavened Bread; this is the
first "historical" mention of the feast, just as "the Moses and they" [1]
narrative marks the first "historical" mention of the Sabbath observance. Now if the "Moses and they" narrative belongs together
with Josh 5, 10-12 as we suggest, then there ought be further indication of this relationship aside from style. Surprisingly enough,
such indication is forthcoming in more or less exact chronological
and textual order in Lev 23, 3-8:

v 3: Six days shall work be done; but on the seventh day is a Sabbath
of solemn rest, a feast day; [2] you shall do no work; it is a
Sabbath to YHWH in all your dwellings.

v 4: These are the appointed feasts of YHWH, the feast days which
you shall proclaim at the time appointed for them.

---

[1] In Josh 5, 10.12 only "the children of Israel" are involved; it seems this
designation is used instead of "they" to link Josh 5, 10-12 with Ex 16, 35,
much like Gilgal is specified in Josh 5, 10 to link our passage to the overall
context, in spite of the mention of the place name in the verse immediately
preceding it.

[2] For this version of מקרא, cf. E. Kutsch, "מִקְרָא," *ZAW* 65 (1953), 247-253.

v 5: In the first month, on the fourteenth day of the month in the evening is YHWH's Passover.

v 6: And on the fifteenth day of that month is the feast of Unleavened Bread to YHWH; seven days you shall eat unleavened bread.

v 7: On the first day you shall have a feast day; you shall do no laborious work.

v 8: But you shall present an offering by fire to the Lord seven days; on the seventh day is a feast day; you shall do no laborious work.

This passage from the Holiness Code seems to have been our "preacher's" choice for his well formulated [1]) halakic midrash. The "Moses and they" narrative comments on Lev 23,3, while Josh 5, 10-12 comments on Lev 23, 5-7. The manna event enters mainly to stress abstinence from laborious work, and not the feasts themselves. By giving or withholding the manna, YHWH taught his people the days of solemn rest, which he himself obviously observed. Thus in accordance with the prescription of Lev 23, 7, the manna ceases (šbt) on the first day of the Unleavened Bread feast, for it is not allowed to do any laborious work on that day. Our preacher comes to an end with his midrash with v 7 of Lev 23, since v 8 does not figure in his discussion.

In short, then, it seems more than likely that Josh 5, 10-12 is closely linked up with Ex 16. What links the two passages, or more specifically, the "Moses and they" narrative and Josh 5, 10-12, is their obvious intent to illustrate the piece of legislation in Lev 23, 3. 5-7. Taken together, the passages form a well-structured midrashic commentary in which the manna serves as an object lesson on solemn rest observances. This lesson is imparted by YHWH himself, who controls the doling out of the manna. With their arrival at the promised land of Canaan, the Israelites are let loose, so to say, to feast upon the produce of the land, with the natural presupposition that the manna lesson will not be lost on them.

---

[1]) As seen from 26, n. 2; 27 nn. 1-3 above (to which add those cited by George, *art. cit.*, 177, n. 31, who would also delete what is lacking in the LXX except the mention of Gilgal), the critics are quite agreed that there are added elements in Josh 5, 10-12; to accede to their suggestions and remove all such additions is much like peeling an onion until nothing is left. Our verses are well structured, relate admirably with Ex 16, and it seems ought not be tampered with except in function with Ex 16.

6) *Summary*

Since the main purpose of this study is to trace the manna tradition it seems opportune at this point to give a summary of that tradition in the Hexateuch in the light of the foregoing analysis. The diagram on the following page points out the main results:

(a) The simple, unamplified tradition is contained in the "Moses and the children of Israel" narrative, which is an aetiological account of the "manna," a food hitherto unknown, given at one period.

(b) Nb 11, 6. 7-9 has "coriander seed" in common with the "Moses and the children of Israel" narrative, but for the rest goes its own way in a manner very similar to the "Moses and they" narrative in its haggadic amplification; the manna comes down.

(c) Dt 8, 3.16 offers a haggadic interpretation of the manna, a food which was not previously known, as the "Moses and the children of Israel" narrative states; manna was used to test the people, as their rejection of it in Nb 21,5 shows.

(d) Finally, the "Moses and they" narrative with Josh 5, 10-12 uses the manna as foundation for a halakic midrash on Lev 23, 3. 5-7, probably basing itself on either the "Moses and the children of Israel" narrative or some such similar account.

B. THE MANNA TRADITION IN PSALMS AND NEHEMIA

1) *Ps* 78, 23-25

The time and place of composition of Ps 78 is a question that has not been adequately settled. [1] However in form and content, the psalm is closely related to the historically based covenant preaching of the Deuteronomist [2] and Chronicles, [3] albeit in poetic form. It takes up the great theme of God's mighty deeds on behalf of Israel of the past and shapes it into a parenesis for Israel of the present. [4]

---

[1] For a discussion and literature, cf. H. J. Kraus, *Psalmen* (Biblischer Kommentar Altes Testament XV/1; Neukirchen, 1961), I, 539-541.

[2] Cf. H. Junker, "Die Entstehungszeit des Ps. 78 und das Deuteronomium," *Biblica* 34 (1953), 493, and G. von Rad, *Studies in Deuteronomy*, 11-24.

[3] Cf. Kraus, *Psalmen*, I, 540, citing von Rad, *Die levitische Predigt in den Büchern der Chronik*, 1934.

[4] Cf. A. Weiser, *The Psalms*, trans. H. Hartwell (Old Testament Library; London, 1962), 538: "The psalm does not present a 'recapitulation of history' or of its main data; its intention is neither to give a chronological outline nor to achieve a kind of synopsis of the relevant historical material. What it wants to portray and impress on the mind is rather 'the riddles from of old' or as we would

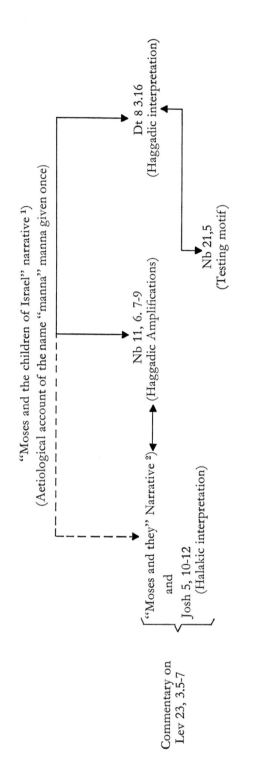

"Moses and the children of Israel" narrative [1]
(Aetiological account of the name "manna" manna given once)

Dt 8 3.16
(Haggadic interpretation)

Nb 21,5
(Testing motif)

Nb 11, 6. 7-9
(Haggadic Amplifications)

"Moses and they" Narrative [2]
and
Josh 5, 10-12
(Halakic interpretation)

Commentary on
Lev 23, 3.5-7

[1] Ex 16, 3ab. 11-15.16b-17a.21.31.35a.
[2] Ex 16, 4abα.5.16a.17b.18-20.22-27.29-30.35b.

In this psalm, the manna tradition receives peculiar treatment, since the psalmist goes his own way in presenting the tradition. Either he fuses various Pentateuch accounts (here Ex 16 and Nb 11) and disregards the Pentateuchal chronology [1]) to prove his point, or he does so because he received the tradition in this way. Our text must be quoted in context:

v 17: But they continued to sin against him,
    to contemn the Most High in the parched land.
v 18: They tested God in their hearts
    by demanding food in their craving.
v 19: And they spoke against God and said:
    Can God spread a table in the desert?
v 20: See, he struck a rock: water flowed and streams welled forth.
    But can he give bread, or provide his people with meat?
v 21: Consequently YHWH heard and grew angry;
    fire flared up against Jacob, (and anger mounted against Israel).
v 22: For they did not have faith in God;
    they did not trust his salvation.
v 23: Then he commanded the clouds above
    and opened heaven's doors.
v 24: He had manna rain down upon them to eat,
    and gave them heaven's grain.
v 25: Man ate the bread of powerful beings;
    he sent them nourishment to the full.

---

say today, the irrational quality of the things that have come to pass in order that present and coming generations will bear in mind and never forget the revelation of God's nature and will together with the nature of human sin; simultaneously they are admonished to be faithful and obedient and warned against unfaithfulness and fickleness so that this knowledge will be preserved as a living force, as the holy tradition of God's covenant." S. Mowinckel, *The Psalms in Israel's Worship*, trans. D. R. Ap-Thomas (New York, 1962), II, 112, considers both our psalms (Pss 78 and 105) as hymnal legends of a didactic character; he writes: "The material is...derived from the history of Israel and the intention is to testify to the faithfulness of Yahweh and the breaking of the covenant on the part of the people, proving the justice of punishment and disaster." With this Weiser would agree, only he sees Ps. 78 "as being uttered by a priest in connection with the tradition of the Covenant festival," (p. 539), and Ps. 105 "as the response of the cult community to the revelation...which had just taken place at the cultic ceremony..." (p. 674).

[1]) Kraus, *Psalmen*, I, 545: "Der Sänger des 78. Psalms verzichtet auf alle vorgegebenen Anordnungen der Tradition, erstrebt keine chronologische Reihenfolge, sondern verknüpft durch selbständig entworfene Übergänge die einzelnen Überlieferungen. So wird eine zur Manna-Erzählung hinführende Überlegung des Volkes unmittelbar an das Felswunder angeschlossen."

v 26: He set the east wind loose in the heavens,
  and drove forth the south wind in his might.
v 27: He had meat rain down upon them like dust,
  winged creatures like the sand of the seas.
v 28: He had them fall in the midst of their camp,
  round about their dwellings.
v 29: Then they ate and became quite filled.
  He brought them what they craved.
v 30: But they did not cease from their craving;
  while their food was still in their mouths,
v 31: (the anger of God mounted against them, and)
  he slew some of their nobles, laying low the chosen of Israel.

In the tradition presented here, or in the interpretation proposed by the psalmist, the manna and quail follow the miraculous event of the water from a rock in the desert. Instead of God testing Israel by the giving of the manna (the interpretation of Dt 8, 3. 16), rather Israel tests God by craving food (the murmuring theme in the "Moses and the children of Israel" narrative of Ex 16), and this testing is described in some detail. Significantly, the Israelites are then fed and felled by God; however the cause of their undoing is not simply craving meat, as in Nb 11, but craving bread and meat, manna and quail. Hence the manna, too, is the cause of their undoing.

As regards the manna itself, God causes it to rain down upon the Israelites (exactly as in the "Moses and they" narrative of Ex 16). But in the psalm, the manna has a rather well-defined point of origin now. It comes directly from heaven through the "šᵉḥaqîm," the clouds that serve as patching pieces holding back the heavenly waters during the annual aging of the firmament, as witnessed by the Palestinian rainy season.[1] Manna is heavenly grain, "dᵉgan-šamayim," and the

---

[1] Cf. H. Torczyner, "The Firmament and the Clouds: Rāqîaᶜ and Sheḥāqîm," *Studia Theologica* I (1947), 190-191: "But what in an European language may be only a single phenomenon of metaphorical speech (i.e. *cloud* derives from *clout*), turned in Hebrew, spoken in Palestine and the neighbouring countries, into a systematic, and as you may say scientific conception of the climatic changes during the year. For here in Palestine the year is divided into two wholly different seasons. During the winter the rains pour down from a sky, torn by storms and covered with clouds; but suddenly clouds and rains cease entirely and the sky is free from its dark covering of rags and clouts. It is as if the sky and its clouds, which the Bible sees as large vessels containing the celestial ocean of 'the waters above the sky,' became torn and worn out after the long and hot summer months. And because these gigantic vessels of water are then torn, until their rags are flying and descending in clouts, the sky apparently must be full of holes and,

bread of the "'abbîrîm," the powerful beings of Ps 103, 20 (where "powerful beings" is parallel with "angels").[1] Thus with Ps 78 the manna takes on a further haggadic trait; it is veritable divine food, occasioning Israel's undoing.

As described in this poetic parenesis, the manna (and the quail, called simply "winged creatures") seems to have come but once. Obviously the psalmist is not interested in the manna in itself. Rather he seizes upon the traditional data of the desert wanderings to point up God's mercy and Israel's continual rebellion. Thus the manna (and quail) is here presented as an item of haggadic midrash; the data is appropriately expanded to help the psalmist prove his point.

2) *Ps* 105, 40

Ps 105 is a cultic hymn, dating from after the Exile, since it presupposes the existence of the Pentateuch in its final, canonical form.[2] Like Ps 78, it is a poetic recitation of the saving events of Israel's past. But instead of being a parenetic sermon that recounts those events, here it is the cultic community's response to God's revelation as represented and actualized in cult.[3] Among these saving events which the community experienced in cult as "a living present reality related to their own lives" [4] stands the manna tradition:

---

through them the rain starts pouring down upon the earth. And who knows, the whole world might be destroyed by another deluge, but for God, who patches up the heavenly bags, thus strengthening them, underlaying a great and strong patch, the rāqîaᶜ. And again for the whole summer-season, the sky stands firm and no drop of rain leaves heaven. Thus, out of this 'scientific' conception of the climatic changes throughout the year, the ideas of the שְׁחָקִים, the clouts or clouds, and רָקִיעַ, the great patch serving as firmamentum for the heavenly water-bags, were born."

[1] Cf. Kraus, *Psalmen*, I, 545: "Man nahm es als die aus Gottes Welt herabkommende Speise auf. Als *lḥm* ʾ*byrym* wird die wunderbare Nahrung in 25a bezeichnet. ʾ*byr* wird im AT Jahwe genannt (Gn 49, 24; Jes 1, 24; 49, 26; 60, 16; Ps 132, 2.5). ʾ*byrym* aber sind hier wohl die himmlischen Wesen, die in Ps. 103, 20 auch *gbry kḥ* genannt werden. Vgl. SapSal 16, 20; 1 Kor 10, 3." Cf. also W. Herrmann, "Götterspeise und Göttertrank in Ugarit und Israel," *ZAW* 72 (1960), 205-216.

[2] Cf. Kraus, *Psalmen*, II, 719: "nicht so sehr ein Lehrgedicht als vielmehr ein Kulthymnus ist... Wenn auch wohl eine Kenntnis des Pentateuchs in seiner kanonischen Endgestalt vorausgesetzt werden muss..." For Mowinckel's view, cf. 31, n. 4 above; Weiser and Kraus are basically in agreement, cf. the following note.

[3] Cf. Weiser, *The Psalms*, 673-674.

[4] *Ibid.*, 675.

v 40: He asked,[1]) and he caused quail to come;
and he sated them with heaven's bread.
v 41: He opened a rock and water welled forth,
it spread over the parched land like a river.
v 42: Because he remembered his hallowed word,
to Abraham, his servant.

The mention of the quail and manna, in that order, is thoroughly
in line with the "Moses and the children of Israel" account of Ex 16.
However here the manna is called heaven's bread or heavenly bread,
"leḥem šamayim," not bread from heaven, "leḥem min-haššamayim."
Perhaps this is due to a tradition similar to Ps 78, or a logical conclusion that bread from heaven must be heavenly bread.

Further, the short passage ascribes the miraculous nourishment to
the intercession of Moses (MT); or if the variant readings be adopted,
to the intercession of Moses and Aaron, or even of the people. The
murmuring motif constantly linked with the giving of the manna is
conveniently forgotten. Finally, the whole line-up of wonderful
events befalling Israel in its exodus from Egypt is linked up with
God's promises to Abraham, his servant. The Exodus and its attend-
ing events are a confirmation of the fact that YHWH struck up an
eternal covenant with Abraham, Isaac and Jacob (vv 7-10). [2])

3) Neh 9, 15.20

Neh 9, 5-37 is presented as a prayer of acclamation of God's
fidelity and goodness on the one hand, and of confession of Israel's
infidelity and perversion on the other. The literary form of this passage is that of a liturgically amplified rîb pattern which includes a
confession of sin and a mention of the mercy of God. [3]) The passage

---

[1]) This is the MT reading, which most commentators and translators emend
to "they asked," blaming the MT reading on haplography, since LXX, Vg,
S and T all have "they asked"; cf. Kraus, Psalmen, II, 718, and Kittel's Biblia
Hebraica (3d ed.), ad versum. The "they asked" would then presumably refer
to Moses and Aaron of v 26, the only "they" mentioned in the context (cf. v 27).
On the other hand, the "he asked" might not be the result of haplography, but
of tendentious interpretation, ascribing the giving of the manna and quail to
the intercession of Moses alone.

[2]) Cf. Kraus, Psalmen, II, 722.

[3]) Cf. J. Vella, La Giustizia forense di Dio (Supplementi alla Rivista Biblica I;
Brescia, 1964), 109-123; the parallels to Neh 9, 6 ff. listed by Vella are: Dan 9,
4-19; Bar 1-3; LXX Dan 3, 26-45; Ps 51. This mention of the mercy of God
in Neh 9 reads much like a parenetic sermon (like Ps 78) rather than like a prayer;

on the mercy of God here (vv 6-35) covers all the salient points of Israel's saving history, from its inception with the call of Abraham. Myers [1]) has aptly noted: "As it stands, the prayer is a composition drawn from many areas, and like Pss lxxviii, cv-cvi, reflects a deep feeling for the nation's historical experiences, as illustrated by the conceptions of the Deuteronomist." Morgenstern [2]) is of the opinion that our passage antedates Ezra, while Rudolph [3]) also inclines to the position that the passage is an insert here. Eissfeldt [4]) considers the Chronicler as the probable author of the prayer. However because of the affinities of our passage with Pss 78 and 106 and the fact that there is almost no trace of P influence as well as no mention of the sin of intermarriage with foreigners, it seems Morgenstern's position is correct. [5])

In our passage, the people in distress (or their spokesman) (v 37) call upon God to stand by them as he did with their "fathers" in the past. In the first half of the prayer, three periods of this divine assistance are recalled: vv 9-12 — at the exodus from Egypt; vv 13-21 — during the desert wanderings; vv 22-25 — at the conquest of Canaan. [6]) Quite naturally, the manna tradition is recorded in the passage on the desert wanderings. Its context is significant:

---

perhaps this is how the LXX interpreted it with its inscription in v 6: καὶ εἶπεν Ἐσδρας, which is lacking in the MT.

[1]) J. M. Myers, *Ezra-Nehemia* (Anchor Bible 14; New York, 1965), 166; cf. 165-170 for literature on the chapter.

[2]) J. Morgenstern, "The Chanukkah Festival and the Calendar of Ancient Israel," *HUCA* 20 (1947), 20, n. 33: "There is cogent internal evidence...that all three (i.e. Neh 9, 5-37; Ps 78 and 106—also the Deuteronomic framework of the Book of Judges) of these compositions come from the period, less than a century in duration, intervening between Deutero-Isaiah and the advent of Ezra, and were written under Deuteronomic litarary and theological influence."

[3]) W. Rudolph, *Ezra und Nehemia samt 3. Ezra* (Handbuch zum Alten Testament; Tübingen, 1949), 157: "Von mehr untergeordneter Bedeutung ist die Frage ob der Chr. das Gebet selbst verfasst oder nur einen bereits formulierten Text aufgenommen hat; da ihm das letztere Verfahren nicht fremd ist (vgl. 1 Chr 16, 8 ff) und er es sonst 'geradezu peinlich vermieden hat, von den Ereignissen der Mosezeit zu sprechen' (Noth Ue. S. 175³), neige ich der zweiten Annahme zu."

[4]) Eissfeldt, *The Old Testament*, 548; on the problem of the order of the book and literature, cf. 541-557, *passim*.

[5]) Cf. Morgenstern, *art. cit.*, 19-20, n. 33, and 21, n. 34: "As is here suggested, Neh 9, 5-37 was originally a part of the established synagogue liturgy of the pre-Ezra period, in all likelihood of Rosh Hashanah, but later in the Chronicler's own day, of Yom Kippur." This position seems sound.

[6]) Cf. H. C. M. Vogt, *Studie zur nachexilischen Gemeinde in Esra-Nehemia* (Werl, 1966), 58-59; Myers, *op. cit.*, 158-164 divides the prayer differently, as does Rudolph, *op. cit.*, 159 ff.

v 13: And you came down upon Mount Sinai, to speak with them from heaven; you gave them right judgments and true torahs, good statutes and commandments.

v 14: You made your holy Sabbath known to them; you commanded them commandments and statutes and torah, through Moses your servant.

v 15: And you gave them bread from heaven for their hunger, and brought forth for them water from the rock for their thirst. And you told them to go and take possession of the land which you swore to give them.

v 16: But they, our fathers, acted haughtily and proved stubborn. They did not obey your commandments;

v 17: they refused to obey and did not remember your wondrous deeds, which you wrought among them;
they were stubborn and in their rebellion appointed a chief to return to their servitude.
But you are a forgiving God, gracious, merciful, patient and abounding in steadfast love; and you did not abandon them.

v 18: Even though they made a molten calf for themselves and said: This is your god, who brought you up out of Egypt; and then showed great contempt,

v 19: yet you, in your abounding mercies, did not forsake them in the desert.
In the daytime the cloud pillar did not stop leading them in the way; nor at night did the fire pillar stop lighting up for them the way in which they were to walk.

v 20: And you gave them your good spirit to instruct them; you did not hold back your manna from their mouths, you gave them water for their thirst.

v 21: And forty years you supported them in the desert; they did not lack. Their clothes did not wear out, and their feet did not swell up.

Significantly, the sequence of events in this prayer is as follows: Exodus (cloud and fire: v 12) — Sinai (laws and Sabbath) — Manna-Water — Golden Calf — cloud and fire — spirit given to elders — Manna-Water. With regard to the manna tradition, the important point here is that the manna is first given after the promulgation of the Sabbath law on Sinai. It is next mentioned after the rebellion marked by the molten calf, which would seem to be the central point of the list of events since it lacks any further parallel. Thus like the "Moses and they" narrative of Ex 16, our passage here presupposes the promulgation of the Sabbath law before the manna is given. But unlike the total Pentateuch narrative, which mentions the manna before and after the Sinai event, our prayer goes its own way.

As far as the manna itself is concerned, like in the "Moses and they" midrash of Ex 16, it is bread from heaven and it is not associated with the quail at all. Further, it is simply food to be eaten i.e. not interpreted in haggadic fahion, and it was available to the Israelites for forty years, as v 21, a free quotation of Dt 8, 4.9, seems to imply.

In conclusion, we might note that if Neh 9, 5-37 is pre-Ezra and not P, then it, or traditions like those contained in it, may be the point of departure for the "Moses and they" narrative of Ex 16.

C. Conclusion

From the foregoing consideration of the manna tradition as presented in the O.T. books of Palestinian origin, we might draw the following conclusions:

1) Aside from the "Moses and the children of Israel" narrative, the haggadic amplifications of Nb 11, 6.7-9 and the casual mention in Nb 21, 5, the manna tradition is always presented in some sort of homiletic or cultic framework.

2) Within this homiletic or cultic framework, the manna tradition undergoes midrashic adaptation, though it is generally always linked up with a complaint or testing in the desert motif (except in Ps 105, the latest composition of all the passages under consideration).

3) The "Moses and they" narrative of Ex 16 along with Josh 5, 10-12 have their point of departure in traditions as presented in Neh 9, 5-37 and Ps 78; hence the diagram on page 32 should be modified. These modifications are shown in the diagram on the following page, which presents a survey of the results of this part of our investigation.

The diagram is not intended to show literary dependencies, but the development of the tradition of the manna into more amplified, midrashic forms. This development begins from the prosaic aetiological account of the name "manna," an account amplified somewhat in Nb 11, 6. 7-9, and then used as a springboard for homiletic ends. In the process the manna takes on admirable traits, ending up as heavenly food, the food of angels,[1] rained down by God upon

---

[1] Herrmann, "Götterspeise und Göttertrank in Ugarit und Israel," 215-216,

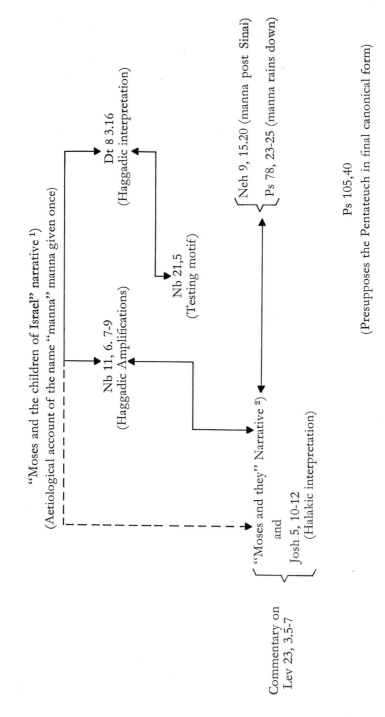

¹ Ex 16, 3ab. 11-15.16b-17a.21.31.35a.
² Ex 16, 4abα.5.16a.17b.18-20.22-27.29-30.35b.

Israel to test and teach the desert generation. The Palestinian exegesis preserved in the Targums continues the development.

---

calls attention to the fact that such amplifications deriving from a common mythological inheritance come to the fore in cult; and we have noted that these midrashic amplifications of the manna tradition are to be found in homiletic or cultic passages. The surprising thing is that these passages are obviously all relatively late, i.e. after the work of the Deuteronomist, hence hardly due to any direct Ugaritic or ancient Canaanite influence. Perhaps they mirror folk tradition, as do many facets of Targumic exegesis.

CHAPTER TWO

THE MANNA TRADITION IN THE PALESTINIAN TARGUMS

In the previous part of this study, we have traced the Palestinian manna tradition up to the end of the O.T. period. In the present chapter we hope to trace the manna tradition into the subsequent period, i.e. the period running from the close of the O.T. to the time of the composition of the Mishnah.[1]) Such a venture is possible mainly due to the extant Palestinian Targums (= PT). [2]) As previously indicated, the manna tradition presented in the O.T. lies thoroughly ensconced within a midrashic framework, and this almost throughout the O.T. Now the midrashic form most closely bound to the O.T. is that of the PT.[3]) The PT form an immediate extension of the O.T., constituting a sort of ligature or bridge between the O.T. and later rabbinic literature.[4]) Hence the most logical place to look for

---

[1]) This period would close, therefore, ca. 200 AD, since the final editor of the Mishnah, Judah ha-Nasi I, died 200 AD; the period corresponds in the main with the period of composition of the intertestamental and N.T. literature.

[2]) The PT referred to in the course of this chapter are the Pentateuch Targums: The Jerusalem Targum (=TJI) cited here from B. Walton (ed.), *Biblia Sacra Polyglotta* (London, 1657) Vol. IV; the Fragmentary Targum (=TJII) cited here from Walton, *ibid.*, and M. Ginsburger, *Das Fragmententhargum* (Berlin, 1899) and the full text of the Fragmentary Targum contained in *Codex Neofiti I* of the Vatican Library (=N), cited here from photographs kindly made available to me by Fr. Roger Le Déaut, C.S.Sp., of the Pontifical Biblical Institute, Rome. The non-Pentateuch Targums used in this study are cited from Walton, *op. cit.*, Vol. III, unless otherwise indicated.

[3]) Perhaps all the extant Targums are of Palestinian origin, including Targum Onkelos (=TO); however our study is not directly concerned with TO for two reasons: first, its literary method is less midrashic than a sort of *peshaṭ*, a simple interpretation of the Pentateuch; second, this interpretation is normally in line with the halakah of the Talmud, hence late; cf. R. Bloch, "Quelques aspects de la figure de Moïse dans la tradition rabbinique,"*Moïse, l'homme de l'Alliance* (Paris, 1955), 96-97, n. 6. The same seems to hold for the Targums to the Prophets ascribed to Jonathan ben Uzziel. For a survey of the opinions on the relationship between the various Targums, cf. G. Vermes, "The Targumic Versions of Genesis IV 3-16," *The Annual of Leeds University Oriental Society* 3 (1961/62), 97-98; and especially R. Le Déaut, *Introduction à la littérature targumique* (Rome, 1966), Part I, 78-123.

[4]) Cf. G. Vermes, *Scripture and Tradition in Judaism: Haggadic Studies* (Studia Post-Biblica IV; Leiden, 1961), 9; R. Bloch, "Note méthodologique pour l'étude de la littérature rabbinique," *RSR* 43 (1955), 211-212; idem,"Quelques aspects..." *art. cit.*, 96-97.

the immediately subsequent interpretations of the manna tradition deriving from the period defined above would be the PT.

Now it is a matter of common knowledge that the extant PT contain exegetical traditions of varying ages; not all the traditions presented in these documents are pre-mishnaic. Further, while N may be pre-mishnaic in the form we have it, the rest of the PT certainly are not.[1]) Therefore the task involved in any use of the PT to trace an O.T. tradition to the pre-mishnaic period is one of literary excavation — to unearth the traditions that are the sole possession of the Targums, or that can be shown to be the basis of later exegetical traditions. In other words, the targumic traditions must be dated.[2])

Consequently, in this part of our study of the manna tradition, we shall first present a translation of the PT to the O.T. texts cited in the previous chapter, followed by an attempt to date the traditions contained in the PT.[3]) In the second section of this chapter, we shall consider the manna tradition as presented in other PT passages. And in conclusion, we shall compare the data preserved in the O.T. with the data handed down in the PT texts. As a result, we should be able to discern the contents of the manna tradition as it existed in the pre-mishnaic period and as preserved in the PT.

A. THE PALESTINIAN TARGUMS TO THE O.T. MANNA TEXTS

1) *Ex* 16

N	TJI
1. Then they left Elim and the whole congregation of the children of Israel came to the desert of Sin which is between Elim and Sinai, on the 15th day of the se-	1. Then they left Elim and the whole congregation of the children of Israel came to the desert of Sin, which is between Elim and Sinai, on the 15th day of *the*

---

[1]) Cf. A. Díez Macho, "The Recently Discovered Palestinian Targum: its Antiquity and Relationship with the Other Targums," *Congress Volume: Oxford* (Supplements to Vetus Testamentum VII; Leiden, 1960), 222-245; *idem*, "Targum," *Enciclopedia de la Biblia* (Barcelona, 1965), VI, 865-881; M. McNamara, *The New Testament and the Palestinian Targum to the Pentateuch* (Analecta Biblica 27; Rome, 1966), 62-66; 112-117.

[2]) For the methodology involved, cf. Bloch, "Note methodologique..." *art. cit.*, 194-227; and especially, Le Déaut, *Introduction à la littérature targumique*, I, 151-181.

[3]) In the following translations, unless noted otherwise, the italicized parts indicate the material not contained in the Hebrew O.T. text (=MT) either in the form presented in the PT or not at all.

cond month from when they were led forth from the land of Egypt.

2. Then the whole congregation *of the assembly* of the children of Israel murmured against Moses and against Aaron in the desert.

3. And the children of Israel said to them: Would that we had died *before YHWH* in the land of Egypt when we sat by the meat pot, eating bread and being filled; but you led us into this desert to kill this whole assembly with hunger.

4. Then YHWH said to Moses: Behold *I will make descend* for you bread from heaven, and the people will go out and gather a day's fixed amount on a given day, so as to test them whether *they are keeping the commandments of the* Law or not.

5. And on the 6th day, *they shall set aside* what they will have brought in, and it shall be twice the daily fixed amount they can gather on a given day.

6. So Moses and Aaron said to all the children of Israel: In the evening you shall know that YHWH led you forth *free men* from the land of Egypt.

month of Iyyar, that was the second month from their departing from the land of Egypt.

2. *And on that day the food which they brought out from Egypt ran out*, and all the children of Israel murmured against Moses and against Aaron in the desert.

3. And the children of Israel said to them: Would that we had died *by the word of YHWH* in the land of Egypt when we sat by the meat *pots*, when we ate bread and were filled; but you have led us into this desert to kill this whole assembly with hunger.

4. Then YHWH said to Moses: Behold *I will make descend* for you *the* bread from heaven *which has been hidden away for you from the beginning*, and the people will go out and gather a day's portion on a given day, in order to test them whether *they are keeping the commandments of* my Law or not.

5. And on the 6th day, when they shall prepare what they will have brought in *for themselves to eat on the day of the Sabbath, they shall lay an 'Erub in their houses and they shall form a Shittuf in their dwellings because of those carrying things about*, and they will have twice as much as they daily gather.

6. So Moses and Aaron said to all the children of Israel: In the evening you shall know that YHWH led you forth *free men* from the land of Egypt.

7. And in the morning you shall see the glory *of the Shekinah* of YHWH, for your murmurings were heard before YHWH, and we, what are we *reputed* to be that you murmur against us? [1]

8. Then Moses said: *Just as* your murmuring, which you are murmuring against him, is heard before YHWH, *so also* will YHWH give you flesh to eat in the evening and bread to the full in the morning; so then *we*, what are we *reputed* to be? Your murmurings are not against us, but they are *before* YHWH.

9. Then Moses said to Aaron: Say to the whole congregation of the children of Israel: Draw near before YHWH, for your murmuring *has been heard* before YHWH.

10. And as Aaron spoke with the whole congregation of the children of Israel, *they paid attention* to the desert, and behold the glory *of the Shekinah* of YHWH appeared in the cloud.

11. And YHWH spoke with Moses saying:

12. The murmuring of the children of Israel has been heard before me. Speak to them saying: At twilight you shall eat flesh and in the morning you shall be filled

7. And in the morning, the glory *of the Shekinah* of YHWH *will be revealed* to you, for your murmurings before YHWH were heard before him; and we, what are we *reputed* to be that you murmur against us?

8. Then Moses said: *In this you shall know*, when YHWH *shall have prepared* for you meat to eat in the evening and bread to the full in the morning, that your murmurings which you are murmuring against him have been heard before YHWH; for *we*, what are we *reputed* to be? Your murmurings are not against us, but rather against *the word* of YHWH

9. Then Moses said to Aaron: Say to the whole congregation of the children of Israel: Draw near before YHWH, for your murmurings *have been heard* before him.

10. And as Aaron was speaking with the whole congregation of Israel, they turned facing the desert, and behold the glory *of the Shekinah* of YHWH appeared in the cloud *of glory*.

11. And YHWH spoke with Moses saying:

12. The murmurings of the children of Israel have been heard before me. Speak with them saying: At twilight you shall eat flesh and in the morning you shall

---

[1] TJII: and we, what are we *reputed* to be.

with bread, and you shall know that I am YHWH your God.

13. In the evening, quail came up and covered the camp; and in the morning there was a *cloud-gathering* of dew round about the camp.[1]

14. Then the *cloud-gathering* of dew went up, and behold upon the surface of the desert, powdery stuff, spread out like hoarfrost upon the ground.[2]

15. When the children of Israel saw, they said to each other: Is this manna? because they did not know . . .[3] Then Moses said to them: This is the bread which YHWH gives you to eat.

16. This is the thing that YHWH commands: Gather of it each one as much as he can eat, an omer per head according to the number of your persons; you shall take each according to how many are in his tent.

17. And the children of Israel did so, and they gathered, some more and some less.

18. Then they measured by the omer, and whoever had more had none left over, and whoever had

eat bread, and you know that I am YHWH your God.

13. In the evening quail came up and covered the camp; and in the morning there was a *sacred* dew*fall arranged like tables* round about the camp.

14. Then *clouds came up and dropped manna upon the dewfall,* and it was finely *levelled out* over the surface of the desert, finely like hoarfrost on the ground.

15. When the children of Israel saw, *they were astonished* and said to one another: *what* is this? because they did not know what it was. Then Moses said to them: This is the bread which *has been hidden away for you from the beginning in the high-heavens,* and *now* already YHWH gives it to you to eat.

16. This is the thing that YHWH commands: Gather of it each one as much as he can eat, an omer per head according to the number of your persons; you shall take each according to the *given amount of men* in his tent.

17. And the children of Israel did so, and they gathered *the manna,* some more and some less.

18. Then they measured by the omer; nothing was left over from the *measure* of those *who*

---

[1] TJII Ginsburger 105: a dewfall.

[2] TJII: like hoarfrost; TJII Ginsburger 105: like hoarfrost on the ground.

[3] Codex Neofiti I has: "because they did not know Moses and Moses said"— obviously a scribal error.

less did not lack — they gathered each as much as he could eat.

19. Then Moses said to them: No one shall leave any of it over till morning.

20. But they did not listen to Moses; and some men left some of it over till morning, and it bred worms and it stank; and Moses grew angry with them.

21. And they gathered it *every* morning by morning, each one as much as he could eat; and when the sun *arose over it*, it melted.[1]

22. And on the 6th day, they gathered bread in double amount, two omers *per head*, and all the *chiefs* of the congregation came and informed Moses.

23. Then Moses said: This is *the thing* that YHWH has said: Tomorrow is the Sabbath of solemn rest, holy before YHWH; what you will bake, bake; and what you will boil, boil; and what is left over, set aside for yourselves to be kept until the morning.

gathered more, and nothing was lacking from the *measure* of those *who gathered* less — they gathered each as much as he eat.

19. Then Moses said to them: No one shall leave any of it over till morning.

20. But they did not *obey* Moses, and *Dathan and Abiram*, *sinful* men, left some of it over until morning, and it bred worms and stank; and Moses grew angry with them.

21. And they gathered it *from* morning-*time till the 4th hour of the day*, each one as much as he could eat, and *from the 4th hour on*, the sun grew hot *over it*, and it melted; *and it became fountains of water which flowed to the great sea, and clean animals and beasts came and drank of it, and the children of Israel hunted and ate them.*

22. And on the 6th day, they gathered bread in double amount, two omers per each *man*, and all the *chiefs* of the congregation came and informed Moses.

23. Then Moses said to them: This is what YHWH said *you are to do*: Tomorrow is the solemn rest of the Sabbath holy before YHWH; what *you have to* bake *tomorrow*, bake *today*; and what *you have to* boil *tomorrow*, boil *today*, and all that is left over *from what you eat today*, set it aside to be kept until the morning.

---

[1] TJII: it melted; TJII Ginsburger 105: and when the sun grew hot, it melted.

24. And they set it aside until the morning as Moses commanded, and it did not stink, and there was no worm in it.

25. And Moses said: Eat it this day, for this day is a Sabbath before YHWH; this day you shall not find it on the surface of the field.[1]

26. Six days you shall gather it, but on the 7th day, the Sabbath, there shall be none *of it*.

27. But on the 7th day, some of the people went out to gather, and they did not find.

28. Then YHWH said to Moses: How long do you refuse to keep my commandments and the *ordinances of my judgments*?

29. See! Because YHWH has given you the Sabbath, therefore he *gave* you on the 6th day bread in double amount; remain each one in his place; no one go out from his place on the 7th day.

30. And the people rested on the 7th day.

31. And the *children* of Israel called its name manna; and it was while like coriander seed, and its

24. And they set it aside until the morning as Moses commanded, and it did not stink, and there was no worm in it.

25. And Moses said: Eat it this day, for this day is the Sabbath before YHWH; this day you shall not find it in the field.

26. Six days you shall gather it, but on the 7th day, *which is* the Sabbath, *the manna* will not *fall*.

27. But on the 7th day, some of the *wicked* people went out to gather *manna*, but they did not find.

28. Then YHWH said to Moses: How long do you refuse to keep my precepts and my *Law*?

29. See! Because YHWH has given you the Sabbath, therefore he gives you on the 6th day bread for two days; remain each one in his place; *do not carry anything from place to place except for 4 cubits*; and no one go out from his place *to walk except for 2000 cubits* on the 7th day.

30. And the people rested on the 7th day.

31. And the house of Israel called its name manna; and it was white like coriander seed, and its

---

[1] TJII Ginsburger 105-106 has the following gloss: "From this day I know that a son of Israel was guilty of eating three times on the Sabbath: once in the evening, once in the morning, and once at twilight, even if indeed there was no difference in the food to eat."

taste was like cakes (made of boiled lentil impregnated) with honey.[1])

32. Then Moses said: This is the thing that YHWH commands A full omer of it is to be kept for your generations, so that they might see the bread which I fed you in the desert upon my leading you forth *free men* from the land of Egypt.

33. So Moses said to Aaron: Take one jar and put inside it a full omer of manna, and put it up before YHWH *in the testimony*, to be kept for your generations.

34. As YHWH commanded Moses, thus did Aaron put it up before the testimony to be kept.

35. And the children of Israel ate the manna forty years, until they entered the land *of their settlement*; they ate the manna until they entered the boundaries of the land of Canaan.

36. The omer is one tenth of *three se'ahs.*

taste like wafer-cakes in honey.

32. Then Moses said: This is thing that YHWH commands: *to reserve* a full omer of it to be kept for your generations so that *the rebellious generations* might see the bread which I fed you in the desert when I led you forth from the land of Egypt.

33. So Moses said to Aaron: Take one *clay* jar and put in it a full omer of manna; put it up before YHWH to be kept for your generations.

34. As YHWH commanded Moses, thus did Aaron put it up before the testimony, to be kept.

35. And the children of Israel ate the manna forty years *in Moses' lifetime*, till they came to inhabited land; they ate the manna *forty days after his death*, till they *crossed the Jordan and* entered the boundaries of the land of Canaan.

36. The omer is one tenth of *three se'ahs.*

A perusal of the foregoing texts easily points up the similarities as well as the differences between them. While N is a more or less faithful rendering of the MT, TJI is a repository for all sorts of halakic and haggadic traditions. However if we prescind from the typical targumic traits [2]) and the accretions proper to TJI, the basic

---

[1]) TJII: white like coriander seed, and its taste like wafer-cakes in honey; TJII Ginsburger 106: like wafer-cakes in honey; another readings: like cakes (made of boiled lentil impregnated) with honey.

[2]) These targumic traits derive from "an endeavor to maintain, as it were, a respectful distance in speaking of God." The description is that of J. F. Stenning, "Targum," *Encyclopedia Britannica* (London, 1960), XXI, 810; there he gives a

difference between the Targums and the MT is that the Targums offer a smoother flowing text. The rough spots left in the MT due to the fusion of the four narratives in Ex 16, singled out in Chapter One, are levelled out.

This smoother rendering is apparent in v 8. The MT is an incomplete sentence. N rectifies the situation by making it a comparative sentence, with כד ··· כד before each member. TJI, on the other hand, links v 8 to v 12 by beginning Moses' statement in v 8 with "in this you shall know." While N is as frugal as MT in the use of the word "manna," TJI uses it freely where necessary to clarify and facilitate the rendition (vv 17, 26, 27). Finally both N and TJI add facilitating clarifications which do not seem to derive from exegetical interests, e.g. "reputed" in vv 7 and 8; "over it" in v 21; "chiefs" in v 22.

a) Halakic elements in the texts

As previously indicated, Ex 16 as it now stands in the MT has as its aim to inculcate the observance of the Sabbath; the manna tradition is put to service as an object lesson to this end. TJI, in turn, uses the Sabbath references in the chapter to pass on some of the current Sabbath legislation, while N lacks any such reference. The way in which these bits of halakoth are interwoven in TJI is a fine example of the way the Targums had served both to keep the people abreast of the latest in rabbinic legislative interpretation as well as how such halakoth were in fact promulgated among the people. In the context of Ex 16, such legislation has the force of Mosaic law.

---

short list of the peculiarly targumic traits. These include: "(1) the insertion of 'word,' 'glory,' 'presence,' before the divine name, when God is referred to in his dealings with men; (2) the insertion of the preposition 'before' when God is the object of any action; (3) the use of the passive for the active voice; (4) the use of periphrasis for the more pronounced anthropomorphisms, such as 'to smell,' 'to taste'; (5) the use of different expressions, or the insertion of a preposition before the divine name, when God is compared to man, or the same action is predicated of God and man." He lists also the peculiar way of treating the divine name and the word 'god' when referring to a pagan god. We might mention here that while it offers many excellent observations, Stenning's article is too Dalman-oriented; for a more up-to-date view of the Targums, cf. P. Kahle, "Das palästinische Pentateuchtargum und das zur Zeit Jesu gesprochene Aramäisch," *ZNW* 49 (1958), 100-116; Díez Macho, "Targum", *art. cit.*, 865-881; M. McNamara "Targumic Studies," *CBQ* 28 (1966), 1-19 = the first chapter of his *The New Testament and the Palestine Targum to the Pentateuch*, 5-37; Le Déaut, *Introduction à la littérature targumique*, I.

Thus in TJI, v 5 tells of the use of the 'Erub [1]) and the Shittuf [2])
practice, while v 29 specifies the Sabbath carrying limit of 4 cubits
and the Sabbath walking limit of 2000 cubits. The halakoth laid
down here represent the pre-mishnaic Pharisaic position, and this
for several reasons. In the first place, the Dead Sea Covenanters [3]) as
well as the book of Jubilees [4]) are clearly against the idea of carrying
about anything at all from one place to another on the Sabbath, hence
against the 4 cubit carrying limit and the Shittuf practice which derives
from it. Likewise, their Sabbath walking limit allowed for only 1000
cubits with one exception, [5]) and hence no room for the 'Erub
practice.

On the other hand, the Mishnah nowhere puts forward a direct
statement of what the Sabbath limits are. Rather all the mishnaic
discussions presuppose the 'Erub and Shittuf practices as well as
the general norm of 4 cubits for carrying and 2000 cubits for walking.
M. Shabbath and M. 'Erubin both take the general norms for granted

---

[1]) H. Danby, *The Mishnah* (Oxford, 1933), Appendix I, 793, describes the
'Erub as follows: "Lit. 'mixture,' 'amalgamation' or 'combination.' (a) According
to the Sabbath Law the movements of the people of a town are restricted on the
Sabbath to 2000 cubits from the boundaries of the town. But if enough food for
two meals is deposited in an accessible place on the eve of the Sabbath at the
prescribed 2000 cubits' distance, this spot counts as a man's temporary abode,
thereby allowing him a range of 2000 cubits beyond the common Sabbath limit.
(b) Similarly 'Erub may be arranged as between the various domiciles within a
courtyard; if all the occupants have a share in a deposit of food placed in a
known place in the courtyard, they are all thereby given unrestricted access to
the premises of the other occupants."

[2]) *Ibid.*, 796, Danby describes the Shittuf thus: "Lit. 'association,' 'partnership.' A deposit of food is placed jointly by the occupants of neighbouring
premises and courtyards in an accessible place in some alley-way. This, for
purposes of the Sabbath law, creates a 'partnership,' thereby granting each
participator access to the premises of the other participators, so effecting a certain
elasticity in the Sabbath restriction which forbids a man to carry a burden from
one domain into another. The areas and premises belonging to those participating
in the Shittuf are thus transformed into a single domain."

[3]) CDC XIV, 30: "Let no man take out (on the Sabbath) anything from the
house outside, or from outside into a house"; and cf. XIV, 31-34; cited from
C. Rabin, *The Zadokite Documents* (Oxford, 1958), 54-55.

[4]) Jubilees 2,30: "And they shall not bring in nor take out from house to house
on that day (i.e. Sabbath)," cited from R. H. Charles, *The Apocrypha and Pseudepigrapha of the Old Testament in English* (Oxford, 1913), II, 15.

[5]) CDC X, 21: "Let him not walk about outside his town above 1000 cubits";
the exception allowing 2000 cubits to a man going to pasture his cattle is stated
in CDC XI, 5-6 (Rabin, 52 & 54); cf. also 1QM 7, 6-7, in Y. Yadin, *The Scroll
of the War of the Sons of Light against the Sons of Darkness* (Oxford, 1962), 290 and a
discussion of this passage on 73-76.

and employ them as points of departure for further elucidations. Further both our vv are cited in the Mekilta [1]) as the loci classici for the halakoth appended to them in TJI, a practice followed likewise by the Talmud compilers for v 29.[2]) And in both the Talmuds and the Mekilta passages, the interpretation of v 29 is anonymous, hence presumably pre-mishnaic in a case of halaka.[3]) Finally, the editor of the Mishnah himself or the tradition he sums up views v 29 as the basis for the Sabbath limits set forth in TJI, as the *incipit* to M. Shabbath shows.[4]) Hence from the evidence available, it would seem that the halakoth in vv 5 and 29 are certainly pre-mishnaic.[5])

As for v 23, the items it enjoins as to be performed before the Sabbath (i.e. boiling and baking) are also presupposed by the Mishnah,[6]) while the whole tenor of the targumized verse readily fits pre-mishnaic practice. [7])

In v 21, TJI specifies that the manna began to melt at the 4th hour, i.e. 10 A.M. This piece of information derives from R. Ishmael (110-130 AD), [8]) and was then taken up by R. Judah (130-160 AD) and

---

[1]) Mekilta on 16, 5 and 16, 29 cited from H. S. Horovitz (ed.) with I. A. Rabin, *Mechilta d'Rabbi Ismael cum variis lectionibus et adnotationibus* (Corpus tannaiticum III/1; Frankfurt, 1931), 161-2 and 170.

[2]) J. ʿErubin IV, 1 cited from M. Schwab, *Le Talmud de Jérusalem* (Paris, 1932), IV, 237; ʿErubin 51a cited from I. Slotki, ʿ*Erubin*: in I. Epstein (ed.), *The Babylonian Talmud: Moʿed II* (London, 1938), 353.

[3]) This presumption derives from the fact that nearly all the halakoth from the time of the Temple are anonymous; hence conversely any authoritative halakah cited anonymously would be from the time of the Temple, mainly because the authors of halakic traditions had to be cited by name; for the evidence and a discussion, cf. B. Gerhardsson, *Memory and Manuscript: Oral Tradition and Written Transmission in Rabbinic Judaism and Early Christianity*, trans. E. J. Sharpe (Acta Seminarii Neotestamentici Upsaliensis 22; Lund-Copenhagen, 1961), 130-131; A. Finkel, *The Pharisees and the Teacher of Nazareth* (Arbeiten zur Geschichte des Spätjudentums und Urchristentums 4; Leiden, 1964), 90-93.

[4]) M. Shabbath I, 1 cited from W. Nowack, *Schabbat (Sabbat)*: in G. Beer, O. Holtzmann, I. Rabin (eds.), *Die Mischna* (II/1; Giessen, 1924), 28 and n. 1.

[5]) Rabin, *The Zadokite Documents*, 53 notes that the 2000 cubit walking limit is historically attested to by the 'boundary' stones of Gezer and in Acts 1, 12; cf. also S. T. Kimbrough Jr., "The Concept of Sabbath at Qumran," *Revue de Qumran* 5 (1966) 483-502, who points out that the origins of the ʿErub practice date from ca. 90 AD, i.e. post-Qumran.

[6]) M. Shabbath VII, 2 (Nowack, 68) mentions kneading and baking, but not boiling, though this is presupposed in the various articles on cooking.

[7]) Cf. CDC X, 22 (Rabin, 53); Jubilees 2, 29; 50, 6 (Charles, II, 15 and 82).

[8]) J. Berakoth IV, 1 (Schwab, I, 72); in the Mekilta on 16, 5 (Horovitz, 161-162) and Berakoth 27a (cited from M. Simon, *Berakoth*: in I. Epstein (ed.), *The Babylonian Talmud: Zeraʿim* (London, 1948), 163) this opinion is cited as anonymous. The English spelling of the names of the rabbis follows that given in the index

applied to the time available for praying the morning tefillah.[1]) Hence while the targumic exegesis was originally a piece of pre-mishnaic haggada, it ended up as basis for a mishnaic halakic position.

b) Haggadic elements in the texts

i) *Elements common to N and TJI*

There are only two haggadic interpretations common to N and TJI in the chapter under consideration. They are to be found in vv 4 and 6. In v 4, the Hebrew המטיר — to cause to rain, is rendered in both PT by מחית, the Aphel of נחת — to make descend, send down. This word and its Hebrew equivalent, ירד, are quite standard in rabbinic literature for references to Ex 16, 4, allowing for some interesting haggadic elaborations.[2]) The problem is whether the PT

---

volume of the English version of the Babylonian Talmud, compiled by J. Slotki (London, 1952); the dates in parentheses after the name of a rabbi indicate his period of activity, unless noted otherwise.

[1]) M. Berakoth IV, 1 cited from O. Holtzmann, *Berakot* (*Gebete*): in G. Beer, O. Holtzmann (eds.), *Die Mischna* (I/1; Giessen, 1912), 60 and n. 1.

[2]) Cf. Tg Ps 78, 24; Mekilta on 16, 4 (Rabban Simeon b. Gamaliel—130-160 AD); on 16, 14 (R. Eleazar of Modi'im—90-130 AD; anonymous; R. Tarfon—90-130 AD) (Horovitz, 160-161 and 165-166); Exodus R. 25, 2.6; 38, 4 cited from S. M. Lehrman, *Exodus*: in H. Freedman, M. Simon (eds.) *Midrash Rabbah* (London, 1939) III, 302, 307, 452; Deuteronomy R. 10, 4 cited from J. Rabbinowitz, *Deuteronomy*: ibid., VII, 168. P. Borgen, *Bread from Heaven: an Exegetical Study of the Concept of Manna in the Gospel of John and the Writings of Philo* (Supplements to Novum Testamentum X; Leiden, 1965), 7-8 cites the haggada of Rabban Simeon b. Gamaliel from the Mekilta on 16, 4 referred to above; the text runs: "Come and see how much beloved the Israelites are by him by whose word the world came into being. Because they are so much beloved by him, he made for them a change in the natural order of things. For their sake he made the upper region like the lower and the lower like the upper. In the past the bread came up from the earth and the dew would come down from heaven, as it is said: 'The earth yielding corn and wine; yea his heavens drop down dew' (Dt 33, 28). But now things have changed. Bread began to come down from heaven, and the dew came up from the earth, as it is said: 'Behold I will cause bread to rain from heaven,' and it says: 'And a layer of dew came up' (Ex 16, 14)"; cf. the shorter parallel in Exodus R. 38, 4 (Lehrman, 452). Borgen also cites Exodus R. 25, 2.6 as verbal parallels. There are two Rabban Simeon b. Gamaliel's generally listed, one belonging to the first generation of Tannaim, the second to the third generation; we attribute the Mekilta haggadah to a third generation Rabban Simeon b. Gamaliel because the existence of two Rabban Simeon's has been seriously questioned by Marti in K. Marti and G. Beer, *Abot* (*Väter*): in G. Beer, O. Holtzmann (eds.) *Die Mischna* (IV/9; Giessen, 1927), 30-33. In any event, the haggada is pre-mishnaic. It further has the merit of deriving solely from considerations of Ex 16—it is the manna and the dew of this chapter that are contrasted. However

interpretation antedates the common rabbinic usage or derives from it. That it had official rabbinic sanction is indicated by its use in TO.[1]) A possible reason motivating the adoption of "to send down" instead of "to cause to rain" here is to obviate a contradiction. After all, the manna does not rain down, but comes down with the dew; and the dew does not rain.[2]) מטר and טל seem to be an impossible Hebrew collocation.[3]) On the other hand, the expression may derive from the influence of Nb 11, 9, where the manna is said to "come down" (ירד).

Be that as it may, it seems certain that the targumic interpretation does preceed the Tannaim, or at least is contemporary with the earliest of them. The evidence comes from Flavius Josephus, who certainly used some sort of Aramaic version of the Pentateuch.[4]) In his treatment of the manna incident in the *Jewish Antiquities*,[5]) he repeatedly refers to the manna as being "sent down," using variants of the word καταπέμπω.[6]) And καταπέμπω is a reliable version of the Aramaic נחת in the Aphel. Josephus, then, is adequate witness to the existence of this N and TJI interpretation of v 4 in early pre-mishnaic times; the usage probably derives from a PT known to him. Pre-

---

the same cannot be said of the traditions cited from Exodus R. 25, 2.6 and treated as of equal value with those of the Mekilta by Borgen. Aside from the fact that the Mekilta antedates Exodus R. as a compilation by some seven or eight centuries (cf. Lehrman, *op. cit.*, vii; O. Lehmann, "Aggadah," *Enciclopedia de la Biblia* (Barcelona, 1963), I, 215-217), the Exodus R. texts offer a homiletic contrast of the manna and the well. In other words, it seems that Rabban Simeon's considerations derive from an exegetical interpretation of "hamṭîr" meaning to cause to send down while the traditions in Exodus R. derive from a contrast between the manna and the well, the word "hamṭîr" not being interpreted but simply taken in its literal sense of to cause to rain like water. Hence while superficially the same, it seems that both traditions are basically different.

[1]) Cited from A. Sperber, *The Bible in Aramaic* (Leiden, 1959), Vol. I.

[2]) Cf. S. Mandelkern, *Veteris Testamenti Concordantiae* (Graz, reprint of 1937), I, 443 for the texts in which "dew" is used.

[3]) "A collocation is the 'lexical company' that a particular lexical item keeps"; J. C. Catford, *A Linguistic Theory of Translation: an Essay in Applied Linguistics* (London, 1965), 10.

[4]) Cf. H. St. John Thackeray, *Josephus IV: Jewish Antiquities I-IV* (The Loeb Classical Library; London, 1957), xii-xiii; and especially P. Winter, "Lc 2, 49 and Targum Yerushalmi," *ZNW* 45 (1954), 148-153; Le Déaut, *Introduction à la littérature targumique*, I, 56-58.

[5]) III, 6, 26-32 (cited from B. Niese (ed.), *Flavii Iosephi Opera* (Berlin, 1888), Vol. I, 122-123). The work was completed in 93-94 AD; cf. Thackeray, *op. cit.*, x.

[6]) LXX translates ירד almost predominantly with καταβαίνω; cf. E. Hatch and H. Redpath, *A Concordance to the Septuagint* (reprint; Graz, 1954), II, 727-728; καταπέμπω does not occur.

mishnaic rabbinic usage further bears out the antiquity of this interpretation.

Verse 4b of the PT likewise agree. Like Neh 9, the PT seem to
presuppose that the Law was already known to the Israelites at this
early state of their desert wanderings. Both PT render MT's הלך
with participles — N: נטרינון, TJI: נטרין. TO on the other hand
adheres closely to MT with יהכון, a contracted form of הלך.

Verse 6 offers an example of a most frequent occurence in PT,
but most especially in N, namely the use of the substantive פריקין,
free men, after the verb נפק in the Aphel, with reference to the Exodus.
N also repeats the phrase in v 32. The frequent use of the phrase in
PT indicates the matter deserves further study; but since it does not
directly bear upon the manna tradition, it need not concern us here.

ii) *Elements proper to N*

The single bit of exegesis proper to N is the question of the Israelites upon finding the manna, v 15. The question is translated as
follows:

MT: מן הוא
  N: מנא הוא
TJI: מאן הוא
TO: מנא הוא
LXX: τί ἐστιν τοῦτο
Josephus: τί τοῦτ'ἔστιν

As can readily be seen, TJI, LXX and Josephus are in agreement
against N and TO. However whether this difference bespeaks a
different exegesis or translation on the one hand, or simply a different
form of the same word on the other, is very difficult to decide. The
Mekilta on 16, 15 [1]) and a host of post-talmudic rabbis [2]) interpret מן
or מנא as meaning "ready-prepared food," deriving the form from

---

[1]) Horovitz, 166.
[2]) Cf. J. Buxtorf, *Lexicon Chaldaicum, Talmudicum et Rabbinicum* (Basel, 1640),
1224 ad verbum; also his full article, "Dissertatio de Manna," in B. Ugolino,
Thesaurus Antiquitatum Sacrarum (Venice, 1747), VIII, 589-592; for Rashi, M.
Rosenbaum and A. M. Silbermann, *Pentateuch with Targum Onkelos, Haphtaroth
and Prayers for Sabbath and Rashi's Commentary* (London, 1930), II, 84; and the
late Numbers R. 12, 3 cited from J. J. Slotki, *Numbers I:* in H. Freedman and
M. Simon (eds.), *Midrash Rabbah* (London, 1939), V, 456.

מנה in Dn 1, 5. [1]) Yet the N and TO form may simply be an emphatic form of מן, meaning "who, what." [2])

iii) *Elements proper to TJI*

To begin with, v 2 informs us that on the day the Israelites arrived at the desert of Sin, their food supply ran out. This identical tradition is found in Josephus. He tells us: "For it was now their 30th day on the march; the provisions which they had brought with them were all exhausted." [3]) Josephus, however, makes mention of this fact while the Israelites are still at Elim; for him, the murmuring against Moses likewise begins there. However that both TJI and Josephus are referring to the same tradition is borne out by the mention of the day being the 30th of the march in Josephus and the 15th of Iyyar in TJI. [4]) Hence the TJI tradition that the Israelites brought a month's supply of food along, is a pre-mishnaic one. [5])

The next haggadic comment comes in v 4, where TJI narrates: "I will send down for you the bread from heaven which has been hidden away (איצטנע) for you from the beginning (מן שירויא)." The same comment crops up in v 15, this time on Moses' lips: "This is the bread which has been hidden away (אצטנע) for you from the beginning in the high heavens and now already (מן שירויא בשמי מרומא וכדון) YHWH gives it to you." The word translated here as "was hidden away" is the Ithpeel form of צנע. This word is used in both N and TJI (as well as TO) in the Aphel to translate the Hebrew הניח in our chapter (vv 23, 24, 32, 33, 34), hence with the meaning of "to put away, put up reserve, deposit." But in the Ithpaal/Ithpeel the meaning is basically "to hide," hence "to restrain oneself, to be private, to be hidden." [6]) In rabbinic usage, the primary meaning of

---

[1]) Yet the discussion on the meaning of *man* in Sukkah 39b (I. W. Slotki, *Sukkah*: in I. Epstein (ed.), *The Babylonian Talmud: Moʿed III* (London 1938), 177) cites Dn 1, 5 but makes no mention of the manna.

[2]) Cf. M. Jastrow, *A Dictionary of the Targumim, the Talmud Babli and Yerushalmi and the Midrashic Literature* (New York, 1950), II, 796, ad verbum.

[3]) Ant. III, 1, 3 (Niese, 118).

[4]) This would be 30 days since they left Egypt on the 15th of Nisan; Nisan has 30 days in the Talmudic calendar (to which TJI probably refers in v 1); cf. J. Vernet, "Mes," *Enciclopedia de la Biblia* (Barcelona, 1965), V, 69-71.

[5]) For later rabbinic opinion, cf. the collected references in L. Ginzberg, *The Legends of the Jews* (Philadelphia, 1928), VI, 16, n. 89.

[6]) Jastrow, *A Dictionary of the Targumim etc.*, II, 1293, ad verbum.

the word in all employable forms is "to hide, conceal." [1]) As far as our vv are concerned, Levy [2]) translates simply"to be hidden."

This tradition of the manna hidden away from the beginning in the high heavens seems to be the proper possession of TJI. One part of it is relatively simple to date. As is well known, Apoc 2, 17 tells of τοῦ μάννα τοῦ κεκρυμμένου [3]); thus the tradition of the hidden manna would date at least to the time of the composition of Apocalypse, and hence be pre-mishnaic.

As far as the manna existing from the beginning is concerned, there is a well known and oft-repeated haggada telling about the time when the manna was created. We cite the version given in TJI Nb 22, 28:

> "Ten things were created after the foundation of the world, on Sabbath eve at twilight: the manna, the well, the rod of Moses, the shamir, the ark (of the covenant), the cloud of glory, the mouth of the earth, the writing of the covenant tablets, demons and the speaking mouth of (Balaam's) ass."[4])

The context here in TJI is the last named item, Balaam's ass; the incident reported in Nb furnished the targumist or scribe with an occasion to fit in this haggadic item.

Now from this haggada, it follows that the time of the manna's origin, "the beginning" of TJI Ex 16, 4.15, means the Sabbath eve

---

[1]) Buxtorf, *Lexicon Chaldaicum etc.*, 1928; but Buxtorf translates v 15: "Iste est panis qui repositus est vobis a principio in coelis excelsis," much like Walton's Polyglot: v 4: "vobis est repositus"; v 15: "reservatus est vobis."

[2]) J. Levy, *Chaldäisches Wörterbuch über die Targumim und einen grossen Theil des rabbinischen Schriftums* (Cologne, 1866), II, 333, ad verbum; cf. also Tg Cant 8,2.

[3]) That κρύπτειν only expresses one facet of the meaning of צפן is to be expected in the translation of a word from a Semitic to a non-Semitic language. Peshitto translates κρύπτειν most frequently with ܛܫܐ = Aramaic טשא which means the same as צפן only for טשא the primary meaning is "to hide," with the secondary meaning "to reserve, put away, put up," etc.; cf. Jastrow, *A Dictionary of the Targumim etc.*, I, 558, ad verbum. Besides, the Hebrew who uses a double meaning word can be conscious of both meanings at the same time; his problem, like ours, would come in trying to translate a double meaning word; cf. I. L. Seeligmann, "Voraussetzungen der Midraschexegese," *Congress Volume Copenhagen* (Supplements to Vetus Testamentum I; Leiden, 1953), 158-159.

[4]) Ginzberg, *The Legends of the Jews*, V, 109, n. 99, lists nine other rabbinic sources beside TJI which carry this haggadah; he concludes: "No two of the sources cited exactly correspond with one another in the enumeration of the things which lies on the boundary line between the primordial things and those developed out of them." For an explanation of the lists, cf. Marti and Beer, *Abot* (*Väter*), 126 ff.; J. Israelstam, *Aboth*: in I. Epstein (ed.), *The Babylonian Talmud: Nezikin IV* (London, 1935), 62-65; H. Freedman, *Pesaḥim*: ibid. *Moʿed II* (London, 1938), 264-267.

of creation week, at twilight,[1]) after the foundation (שכליל) of the
world. All this information is certainly pre-mishnaic, probably even
pre-tannaitic. In the first place, the manna is mentioned in the Aboth
listing (M. Aboth V, 6) as well as in all the older rabbinic sources.[2])
These listings were known to the fathers of R. Nehemiah and R.
Josiah, themselves third generation Tannaim; [3]) hence the listings
were certainly in existence ca. 100 AD. Secondly, the rabbinic passages [4]) relating this haggada make no further mention of the time
when the various ten things were created aside from the vague
"on Sabbath eve, at twilight." TJI Nb 22, 28 is the only one of these
to specify: "after the completion of the world." Now this specifi-
cation may derive from the targumic tendency to clarify the implicit
or to distinguish these things from those created before the creation
of the world.[5]) However it seems to be as early as 1 Peter, which
mentions one of the varying ten things,[6]) the ram-lamb (of the
Abraham-Isaac-sacrifice incident in TJI Gen 22, 8) known from
before the foundation of the world (1 Pt 1, 20). [7])

All the items listed in the various versions of the haggada are
things which would require, according to the rabbinic view, immediate creation by God either because miraculous in the course of
Israel's history or because necessary as prototype or instrument (e.g.
the mule, tongs) in later human history in general. The point of
departure for the speculation leading to these lists is not the fact that
the items listed are important in Israel's religious history, [8]) but
rather the principle that God's works were finished from the time

---

[1]) Literally, "between the suns" = בין־השמשות, ביני שימשתא. ביני שימשות. The meaning of
the phrase is much disputed; cf. Marti and Beer, and Israelstam, loc. cit. in the
previous note. R. Le Déaut, "Le Targum de Gen 22, 8 et I Pt 1, 20," RSR
49 (1961), 106, n. 11 observes: "Le texte des Pirqé Abot (V, 6) porte aussi 'entre
les deux soleils', ce qui semble bien être une retraduction de l'araméen, le pluriel
de šemeš n'étant employé dans la Bible qu'en Is. 54, 12, au sens figuré de 'créneaux'."

[2]) For a comparison of those sources, cf. Marti and Beer, Abot (Väter), 126.

[3]) Pesaḥim 54a (Freedman, 264).

[4]) Aboth V, 6; Mekilta on 16, 32; Siphre Deut. 33, 21; Pesaḥim 54a, 54b;
and those cited by Marti and Beer, loc. cit. in n. 2 above.

[4]) Cf. Pesaḥim 54a (Freedman, 265).

[6]) There are 21 items in all in these varying lists of ten things, enumerated
by Ginzberg, loc. cit. in n. 4 on previous page.

[7]) Cf. Le Déaut, "Le Targum de Gen 22, 8 et I Pt 1, 20," art. cit., 103-106.
And compare καταβολή = foundation, beginning (1 Pt 1, 20 and N.T. passim,
only once in LXX 2 Mac 2, 29) and שכליל = foundation, completion, ending
(TJI Gen 7, 11; 22, 8; Nb 22, 28) and שירויא = beginning (in our vv, TJI Ex 16,
4.15).

[8]) Cf. Le Déaut, ibid., 104, n. 6 citing la Bible du Centenaire: "Les Juifs croy-

of the foundation of the world, i.e. the last day of creation week, and since then there is nothing new under the sun.[1]

The final piece of information contained in vv 4 and 15 tells of the place where the manna was hidden away for the Israelites, namely "the high heavens," or "the heavens on high." In Tg Ps 71, 19; 75, 6; and Tg Job 25, 2 the phrase translates the Hebrew: מרום; while in Tg Job 21, 22 it translates רמים. There is a tradition ascribed to Resh Laḳish (ca. 250 AD) in Ḥagigah 12b, [2]) according to which there are seven heavens, and the manna was created in the third of these, the שחקים. [3]) However none of these heavens is called רמים or מרום.[4]) Hence the haggada in TJI Ex 16, 4.15 offers no indication whatsoever of having anything to do with these speculations, and therefore is the proper possession of TJI. The haggadic elements of both vv then would date to the same period, i.e. before the composition of the Apocalypse.

The next haggadic item in TJI comes in vv 13-14; there the Targum tells of "a sacred dewfall arranged like tables," upon which "the

---

aient à la préexistence dans la pensée de Dieu ou dans le ciel, des hommes et même des choses qui jouaient un rôle important dans leur histoire religieuse."

[1]) Cf. Marti and Beer, (Abot (Väter), 127: "Mit der Aufzählung der zehn im Zwielicht vor dem Schöpfungssabbat geschaffenen Dinge und Wesen gibt der Verf. eine Theorie über die in der Schrift erwähnten Wunder. Ausserhalb des regelmässigen Naturlaufes stehend und doch wiederum darin verflochten, sind sie als ein Anhang oder Nachtrag zur eigentlichen Schöpfung, d.h. zur Erschaffung des unverbrüchlichen Weltganzen und seiner Teile, idealiter hervorgebracht, um im rechten Augenblick in die festgefügte Kette des Naturgeschehens, die auf diesen Eingriff schon vorbereitet ist, sich einzureihen. Denn für den gläubigen Juden gilt das Wort Koh 1, 9: Es gibt nichts Neues unter der Sonne. Und wo Gott auch Neues schafft Jes 43, 19; 65, 17ff., geschieht es nach einem ewig vorbedachten Plan." Cf. also Heb 4, 3.

[2]) Cited from I. Abrahams, Ḥagigah: in I. Epstein (ed.), The Babylonian Talmud: Mo‘ed IV (London, 1938), 69. Billerbeck, in H. L. Strack and P. Billerbeck, Kommentar zum Neuen Testament aus Talmud und Midrasch (Munich, 1929), III, 532, ascribes the tradition to R. Meir (ca. 150 AD) on the basis of Aboth de Rabbi Nathan: "Chag 12b: R. Meir (um 150), so lies mit Aboth RN 37 statt 'Resch Laqisch' (um 250)." But Ginzberg, The Legends of the Jews, V, 10, n. 22 questions Aboth de Rabbi Nathan instead of the Talmud: "That the idea concerning the seven heavens originated in the Tannaitic period cannot be definitely proved. It is found in a statement by R. Meir (ARN loc. cit.), but the authenticity of this source is not above suspicion."

[3]) The word clearly derives from Ps 78, 23 and is used to designate the locus of the manna's origin since the verb שחק means, among other things, to grind up, and the manna was ground up; cf. the article by H. Torczyner, cited on p. 34, n. 1 above. In Mekilta on 16, 13, R. Eleazar of Modi‘im (90-130 AD) has the manna falling from the firmament (רקיע) (Horovitz, 165).

[4]) The list in Abraham's transcription: "Wilon, Raḳia‘, Sheḥaḳim, Zebul, Ma‘on, Makon, ‘Araboth," loc. cit. n. 2 above.

clouds came up and dropped manna." This explanation seems to derive from the double meaning of the Aramaic אנחותא, used here to translate TM שכבא. The Aramaic word means both "fall, descent," [1] and "table, platter." Thanks to this double meaning and the exegesis it allows for, the tannaitic rabbis combined it with Ps 78 and developed some interesting conclusions. To cite just one example, R. Eliezer (90-130AD) said:

> "How did the manna come down to the children of Israel? The northwind would blow and sweep clean the desert surface, then rain would fall and wash the earth; then the dew would go up and the wind blow over it and make it into a sort of table of gold. Then the manna would fall upon it." [2]

However none of the rabbinic haggadoth relating this miraculous preparation of a table in the wilderness refer to the dew as טלא מתקדשא, sacred or sanctifying. This attribute either bespeaks speculation about the nature of the dew or simply aims to point out its divine or miraculous character.[3]

Other clarifications embedded in the TJI Ex 16 text which probably derive from rabbinic homilies are the characterizations of the Israelites who proved disobedient at the time the manna was given. The disobedient are indicated either by name — thus the infamous pair "Dathan and Abiram, sinful men" [4] (cf. TO Nb 16, 25-26) emerge in v 20 — or by attribute implying moral judgment — the wicked in v 27, and the rebellious generations in v 32. Rabbinic sources, from

---

[1]) Jastrow, *A Dictionary of the Targumim etc.*, I, 82, says this word here means "layer," and cites only our two verses. Buxtorf, *Lexicon Chaldaicum etc.*, 1332, does not consider the word "layer," deriving our word from נחת, in the Aphel. As for the word ענות in TJII Ginsburger 105, Jastrow, *ibid.*, II, 1092, follows the Arukh and translates: "a divine supply, grant"; Buxtorf, *ibid.*, 1633, thinks the form in Arukh is erroneous and ought be אנחות with TJI.

[2]) Mekilta on 16, 13 (Horovitz, 165); Mekilta on 16, 14 (Horovitz, 165) also contains an identical haggada ascribed to Eliezer's contemporary, R. Joshua. Finally, the same tradition is found in Midrash on Ps 78, 3 cited from W. G. Braude, *The Midrash on Psalms* (Yale Judaica Series XIII/2; New Haven, 1959), II, 24-25; cf. Ginzberg, *The Legends of the Jews*, VI, 17, n. 100.

[3]) Cf. Josephus, Ant. III, 1, 27 (Niese, 122): ἀνεδίδασκεν οὐ κατὰ τὴν ἐκείνων ὑπόληψιν ἀπ' οὐρανοῦ καταφέρεσθαι τὴν δρόσον, ἀλλ' ἐπὶ σωτηρίᾳ τῇ αὐτῶν καὶ διατροφῇ.

[4]) In Exodus R. 25, 10 (Lehrman, 313) the linking of Dathan and Abiram with this incident in Ex 16 is ascribed to R. Simeon b. Laḳish, a Palestinian Amora of the 3rd century. In Tanḥuma תצות, 11 (ed. Zundel; Jerusalem, 1960, 114) it is cited without reference by a certain R. Joḥanan. From this evidence, the mention of Dathan and Abiram here in TJI would be late.

the time of the Mekilta on, offer much speculation about this wilderness generation of Israelites, the first to get the manna and the first to break the Sabbath law.[1]

The tradition presented in TJI Ex 16, 21 also seems to be pre-mishnaic. This tradition relates that the manna was not wasted, but "it became fountains of water which flowed to the great sea, and clean animals and beasts came and drank of it, and the children of Israel hunted and ate them." In the rabbinic texts it is the pagan nations who come to hunt these animals, not the Israelites.[2] The origin of this explanation seems to derive from tannaitic speculation on the amount of manna, which was, after all, like hoarfrost and melted. R. Eleazar of Modi'im (90-130 AD), for example, claimed the manna was 60 cubits high.[3] Later the amount increases appreciably.[4]

Interesting from the viewpoint of targumic exegetical procedure is the variant of the translation of MT נתן in v 29. N has יהב (with TO), the Peal perfect, "he gave"; while TJI has יהיב, the Peal participle, "he gives." [5] The emphasis in TJI, then, is placed upon God's continued providence. Again from the viewpoint of targumic tradition, the note on the type of jar in which the omer full of manna was kept (v 33) is of interest. N (with TO) is as neutral as MT. But TJI specifies צלוחית דפחר, an earthenware jar, while LXX has στάμνον χρυσοῦν, a jar of gold. The LXX would reflect the Alexandrian targumic tradition (followed by Heb 9, 4), while TJI, the Palestinian.[6]

---

[1]) Cf. Ginzberg, *The Legends of the Jews*, VI, 18-19, nn. 109 and 110, where the sources are cited along with a discussion.

[2]) E.g. Mekilta on 16, 21 (Horovitz, 168); in other versions of this haggada, the conclusion is different, e.g. as the upshot of their hunting the pagan nations learn of the greatness of Israel (Rashi, ad versum, in Rosenbaum and Silberman, *op. cit.*, 85), and even acknowledge the God of Israel (Leqaḥ Ṭob, cited by Ginzberg, *The Legends of the Jews*, VI, 18, n. 103). To bring the TJI text into harmony with rabbinic tradition, Ginzberg, *loc. cit.*, would emend "children of Israel" to "children of the nations"; but perhaps TJI records another tradition; note that TJI specifies they were "clean" animals.

[3]) Mekilta on 16, 14 (Horovitz, 165); Yoma 76a cited from L. Jung, *Yoma*: in I. Epstein (ed.), *The Babylonian Talmud*: *Moʿed III* (London, 1938), 369-370.

[4]) Cf. Yoma 76a (Jung, 370), Midrash on Ps 78, 3 (Braude, II, 23).

[5]) According to Borgen, *Bread from Heaven*, 63-64, Jn 6, 32 offers an example of a similar sort of verbal alteration for exegetical reasons in a context dealing with manna; Borgen uses the Hebrew *ntn* as a hypothetical analogy; TJI and N offer a factual analogy in Aramaic.

[6]) Cf. Mekilta on 16, 33 (Horovitz, 171) and Ginzberg, *The Legends of the Jews*, VI, 19, n. 111; J. Buxtorf, "Dissertatio de Manna," in Ugolino, *Thesaurus*, VIII, 629-630; and J. Buxtorf Jr., "Historia Arcae Foederis," *ibid.*, 209-212.

The final haggada proper to TJI in Ex 16 is that related in v 35, that the manna kept coming down for 40 years in Moses' lifetime and for 40 days after he died. The exegesis espoused in this passage is that of R. Joshua (90-130 AD).[1]) Hence it is pre-mishnaic. On the other hand, TJI shows itself a repository for traditions of various centuries by carrying a variant contradictory tradition in Dt 34, 7. Instead of 40 days of manna after Moses' death, TJI Dt 34,7 has the following:

> "And the children of Israel wept for Moses on the plains of Moab for 30 days, and the days of mourning-tide weeping for Moses ended on the 8th of Nisan. Then on the 9th of Nisan the people of the house of Israel prepared their vessels and put their beasts in order, and on the 10th of Nisan they passed over the Jordan. Now the manna ceased for them on the 16th of Nisan; they ate the manna because of the merits of Moses 37 days after he died."

According to TJI Dt 32, 48 and most of the Tannaim of the Mekilta,[2]) Moses died on the 7th of Adar. However these rabbis presuppose an Adar of 31 days in their computations, [3]) while the aforecited text presupposes an Adar of 29 days, as in the later Talmudic calendar. Hence TJI Dt 34, 7 is much later than TJI Ex 16, 35, which itself derives from the Tannaim.

To summarize the foregoing considerations of PT Ex 16, all the bits of exegesis preserved in the PT under discussion are demonstrably pre-mishnaic, except for the mention of Dathan and Abiram in v 20. Among the exegetical traditions preserved here, a few are

---

[1]) Mekilta on 16, 35 (Horovitz, 172).

[2]) Mekilta on 16, 35 (Horovitz, 172) reports: "R. Eliezer (90-130 AD) says: ... Moses died on the 7th of Shebat..." The dating of Moses' death on the 7th of Adar (cf. the following note) or 7th of Shebat would derive from the fact that the account of Moses' death was read on these days, in triennial cycle, according to A. Guilding, *The Fourth Gospel and Jewish Worship: a Study of the Relation of St. John's Gospel to the Ancient Jewish Lectionary System* (Oxford, 1960), 29, n. 1.

[3]) Mekilta on 16, 35 (Horovitz, 172): "R. Joshua says:... Moses died on the 7th of Adar, and they ate of the manna 24 days in Adar and 16 in Nisan"; "R. Eleazar of Modi'im says: Moses died on the 7th of Adar and they ate of it 24 days in the first Adar and 30 days in the second, for it was a leap year..." Prescinding from the leap year, the fact is these rabbis have 31 days in the first Adar, not 29 or 30 as in the later talmudic calendar; cf. J. Vernet, "Calendario Judio," *Enciclopedia de la Biblia*, II, 43-46. On the various rabbinic opinions on how long the manna lasted, cf. Buxtorf, "Dissertation de Manna," *art. cit.*, 634-640; this speculation is motivated, it seems, by the fact that the Israelites did not have the manna for 40 complete years according to the chronological indications in the Bible.

certainly either pre-Christian or contemporary with the first Christian generation; these are the following:

(1) v 2: the manna comes just when the supplies Israel brought out of Egypt ran out;

(2) v 4: the manna is sent down from heaven, not simply allowed to rain down;

(3) vv 4, 15: the manna is the bread which has been hidden away or reserved for the Israelites from the beginning in the heavens on high.

Moreover, the traditions on the Sabbath limits (vv 5, 29) and on the nature of the dew that brings the manna as being sacred (v 13) are probably also from the 1st century AD.

2) *Nb* 11, 6-9

N	TJI
6. But now our soul is *empty*; there is nothing at all for us except only (except this manna which our eyes see)[1] up to which our eyes *are lifted*.	6. But now our soul is dried up; there is nothing at all except the manna *which we await like a poor man looking out for* (the left-overs of) *a dish at the hands* (of his master).
7. Now the manna was like coriander seed, and its appearance like the appearance of bdellium.[2]	7. *Woe to the people whose food is the heavenly bread*; *then they would murmur that* the manna was in likeness like coriander seed, *round when it fell from heaven*; *and when it was untouched* its appearance was like the appearance of bdellium.

---

[1] The phrase in parentheses is from a marginal gloss, of a different hand than the text; the text as it stands is incomplete and reads as follows: לית לן כל מן דעם ארום אהין—there is nothing at all for us except אהין; this last mentioned word is probably an abbreviation for אליהין as is usual in Codex Neofiti I (e.g. cf. fol. 288b). However it may be a form of the word אהינא, a species of late and inferior dates (cf. Jastrow, *A Dictionary of the Targumim etc.*, I, 20, ad verbum). The reason for mentioning this possibility here is that in Memar Marqah IV, par. 9 (cited from J. MacDonald, *Memar Marqah: the Teaching of Marqah* (Beihefte zur *ZAW* 84/I-II; Berlin, 1963), I, 104 for text; II, 172 for version) we find that the manna tasted like מעפין בסולך, which MacDonald translates as "sweetmeats," and in the note, "or reddish, dates" with honey.

[2] TJII Ginsberger 114: coriander *white*.

N	TJI

N

8. The people went out and collected and ground and made it into cakes, and its taste was like the taste of *cakes* (made of lentils and impregnated) *with honey*.[1]

9. And when the dew used to come down upon the camp at night, the manna came down upon it.

TJI

8. The *wicked* people *grabbed after and* used to gather and grind in mills, and *whoever wanted to* used to crush in a mortar and boil it in a pot and make cakes of it, and its taste was like the taste of a *brisket interlarded* with oil.

9. And when the dew used to come down upon the camp at night, the manna came down upon it.

As can be seen, there are no common readings in N and TJI which would be at variance with MT. Rather each Targum goes its own way.

i) *Elements proper to N*

The description of the taste of the manna in v 8 (TJII is the same [2]) as well as the reference to its color in TJII (Ginsburger) v 7 both derive from the previous Exodus account. Perhaps the aim of these renderings is to bring both descriptions of the manna into harmony, and thus avoid an obvious contradiction in Scripture, or to indicate that the manna of Nb is the same as the manna of Ex. On the other hand, N and TJII may mirror the early widespread idea that heavenly food is sweet.[3] With their version here, they would thus bring out

---

[1]) TJII: The people used to roam about and gather and grind in mills or crush it in mortars, and they used to boil it in a pot and make cakes of it, and its taste was like the taste of *cakes* (made of lentils and impregnated) *with honey*. TJII Ginsburger 114: or crushed it in mortars... and they cooked in a pot.

[2]) A. Geiger, *Urschrift und Übersetzungen der Bibel in ihrer Abhängigkeit von der innern Entwicklung des Judentums* (2d ed.; Frankfurt/M., 1928), 471 seems to be citing a text of TJII different from ours and N as well; he claims his TJII agrees with TO here, while TO has: "of dough with oil."

[3]) Josephus, Ant. III, 1, 28 (Niese, 122) makes no mention of the taste of oil, only of honey; the same is true of the reference to manna in the legend of Joseph and Asenath (in P. Riessler, *Altjüdisches Schrifttum ausserhalb der Bibel* (Augsburg, 1928), 518 ff.); in the Sibylline Oracles, Fragment III, 49 (in J. Geffcken, *Die Oracula Sibyllina* (Die griechischen christlichen Schriftsteller der ersten drei Jahrhunderte VIII; Leipzig, 1902), 232) manna is called "sweet bread"; this fragment certainly dates before 150 AD, since it is cited by Theophilus of Antioch, *Ad Autolycum II*, 36 (PG 6, 1116). Cf. also Wis 19, 21, and K. Wernicke, "Ambrosia," in F. Pauly, G. Wissowa (eds.), *Real-Encyclopädie der classsischen Altertumswissenschaft* (Stuttgart, 1894), I, 1809-1811.

an idea certainly shared by their audience and thoroughly in line with
the Scriptures (Ex).

ii) *Elements proper to TJI*

Unlike N, TJI offers ample targumic expansion containing traditions certainly of pre-mishnaic origin. To begin with, the lament
at the close of v 6 is a citation of Tg Ps 123, 2.[1]) Whether TJI is
dependent on Tg Ps here or vice-versa cannot be determined with
certainty. However in the present context of TJI, the words intimate
that the complaint of the Israelites derives from uncertainty ("which
we await") of the daily dole of manna, as well as the way in which the
manna is doled out. Josephus [2]) offers a similar interpretation of the
complaint: ". . . and if it should happen that the manna fall short,"
the Israelites would die.

Further, as regards v 7, Ginzberg [3]) rightly notes that the tannaitic
sources [4]) view Nb 11, 7 as the protest of Scripture against the slan-
derous words of Israel in the preceding verse. Josephus [5]) in turn
has one of the people utter the protest: 'someone admonished
them . . .'" Hence both Josephus as well as the anonymous Tannaim
consider v 7 a protest, not merely a description of the manna. But
since the verse itself is no sort of protest, the tannaitic sources presuppose some haggada using this text as a protest, while Josephus
probably read such a protest in the Aramaic Bible he used. Consequently the tradition embodied in our verse of TJI, if not the entire
TJI passage, certainly antedates both the aforementioned sources.

The information that the manna was "round when it fell from
heaven, and when it was untouched (literally: holy)" it was like
bdellium, is probably added to contrast with the following verse;
v 7 simply describes the manna as it was before any culinary changes.

The mention of the wicked people and their grabbing [6]) after the
manna in v 8 is in line with TJI's interest in pointing up the sinfulness

---

[1]) Cf. Jastrow, *A Dictionary of the Targumim etc.*, II, 728.

[2]) Ant. III, 13, 296 (Niese, 165).

[3]) *The Legends of the Jews*, VI, 86, n. 470.

[4]) E.g. Siphre Nb 88 (cited from H. S. Horovitz (ed.), *Siphre ad numeros adjecto
Siphre zutta* (Corpus tannaiticum III/3; Leipzig, 1917), 87-88) for two versions
of the same protest.

[5]) Ant. III, 13, 297 (Niese, 165).

[6]) The word for "to grab after," חפס, has this meaning in Tg Job; generally
it means "to dig," but this meaning does not seem to fit here; cf. Jastrow, *A
Dictionary of the Targumim etc.*, I, 492.

of this desert generation, an interest very apparent in Ex 16. Then
the explanation offered with the phrase, "whoever wanted to," in
the same verse is either a simple targumic expansion, or intended to
offset objections that may have arisen from the widespread haggada
that the manna tasted just like anyone wished it to taste.[1]) For if the
manna had all tastes possible, then why would the Israelites want to
cook, crush, grind and boil it. The targumic addition explains why;
it was up to the people and their own good pleasure.

The final piece of targumic exegesis here deals with the taste of
the manna. MT informs us that the manna tasted like לשד השמן,
probably a type of cake made with oil. The word לשד seems to have
been a difficult one for the early translators. It occurs only twice
in the O.T., here and in Ps 32, 4 where it means "sap, vital juices."
LXX translates it ἐγκρίς,as it does the parallel צפיחית of Ex 16, 31.
This difficulty offers another possible reason for N's translating the
phrase with that of Ex 16, 31. The early rabbis, perhaps to do away
with a difficult word, read it as שד, (female) breast,[2]) and then expanded on how the manna was for the desert generation what the
breast is for a child. This bit of exegesis antedates the earliest datable
rabbinic text (unless R. Jose b. Ḥanina cited in Exodus R V,9 is
the Tanna of the 1st-2nd generation[3]) since it is found already in
Aquila; he renders the word μαστός, breast.[4]) TJI does the same
with the rendering ביזא, pap, breast, brisket. As a result of TJI's version, the rabbinic שד takes on fresh meaning, "a brisket interlarded
with oil," a meaning not as artificial as the Hebrew שד.[5])

In summary, the targumic comments in TJI at the close of v 6 and
the beginning of v 7 would derive from a period prior to Josephus,

---

[1]) The earliest written record of this tradition is Wis 16, 20-21 for Alexandria;
in Palestinian writings, the record comes later, cf. Ginzberg, *The Legends of the
Jews*, VI, 17, n. 99.

[2]) Siphre Nb 89 (Horovitz, 89); Tosephta Soṭah 4, 3 (ed. Zuckermandel, 299)
are both anonymous; Yoma 75a (Jung, 364) quotes R. Abbuha, an Amora;,
Exodus R. 5, 9 (Lehrman, 87) quotes R. Jose b. Ḥanina, either the Tanna or
the Palestinian Amora of the 3rd century, in which case Billerbeck, *Kommentar
etc.*, II, 481, opts for the latter.

[3]) Cf. the previous note.

[4]) Cf. A. Geiger, *Urschrift und Übersetzungen der Bibel*, 471; Geiger states that
later rabbinic tradition (e.g. TO which translates "dough") consistently avoided
the word שד, and replaced it with some euphemistic expression, clear proof of
the antiquity of TJI.

[5]) Cf. Rashi's objection: "but really the subject of 'breasts' has nothing to do
with oil" (Rosenbaum and Silbermann, IV, 54); and Geiger, *op. cit.*, 397 note.

hence contemporary with the N.T. documents. The closing comment on the taste of the manna in TJI would derive at least from the time of Aquila.[1]) The remaining comments in the PT seem to be proper to them, hence dating from the time of the origin of these Targums.

3) *Nb* 21, 5-6

N	TJI
5. Then the people spoke against *the word of* YHWH and grew angry with Moses: Why now did you bring us from Egypt *to kill us* in the desert? For we have no bread *to eat* and no water *to drink*, and we are weary of this bread which is light *food*.	5. Then the people *thought in their hearts and* talked against *the word of* YHWH and *wrangled* with Moses: Why did you bring us up from Egypt to die in the desert? For there is no bread and there is no water, and we loathe this *manna* which is light *food*.
6. *The Bath Qol came forth from within the earth, and its voice was heard on high: Come, see, all creatures, and come, listen, all children of flesh! I cursed the serpent from the beginning and I said to it: Dust shall be your food. I brought up my people from the land of Egypt and I made manna come down from heaven for them, and I made the well come up for them from the deep, and I made quail pass by for them from the sea. Yet they continue to murmur before me because of the manna which is light food. So let the serpent come which did not murmur about its food, and let it bite the people who murmur about their food.* Therefore YHWH let loose fiery serpents among the people, and they bit the people, and many of the people of Israel died.[2])	6. *The Bath Qol fell from the high heavens, and spoke thus: Come, see, all children of men, all the good things that I did for the people whom I brought up free men from Egypt. I made manna come down for them from heaven, and when they continued to murmur against me, then behold, the serpent concerning which I decreed from the days of the beginning of the world: Dust will be his food, and he did not murmur against me. But my people murmur against their food. So therefore let serpents come which did not murmur about their food and bite the people who have murmured about their food.* Therefore *the word of* YHWH let loose *annihilating-basilisk* serpents, and they bit the people, and a great crowd of Israel died.

---

[1]) According to Epiphanus, Aquila's version dates from 128-129 AD; the version is heavily endebted to Aḳiba's influence; cf. D. Barthélemy, *Les Devanciers d'Aquila* (Supplements to Vetus Testamentum X; Leiden, 1963), 15-21.

[2]) TJII: *The Bath Qol came forth from within the earth and the voice was heard on high:*

These texts witness that the tradition of a Bath Qol before God's
punishing the Israelites with serpents for their murmuring is unani-
mous and standard in the PT. The clarifications of v 5, which serves
to introduce the Bath Qol message, basically add nothing special to
the haggada of v 6, since the different manner of speaking about
YHWH and Moses is the usual targumic trait called into play when
both God and a mortal are made the object of the same verb.[1]) Yet
interestingly enough, N quotes v 5 of TJI in its Bath Qol message,
i.e. "the manna which is light food," while TJII quotes v 5 of N, i.e.
"this bread which is light food." These cross-elements certainly point
to a common origin for the haggada of v 6 in the various PT.

As regards v 6, the haggada there seems to be proper to the PT
tradition. Its date would have to be that of the origin of these Targums,
since there is no datable rabbbinic tradition, to our knowledge,
that might serve as a parallel. The only text in some way similar to
it is related in Midrash Tanḥuma: [2])

> "Another reason why he punished them by means of serpents: Even
> if the serpent eats all the delicacies in the world, his food changes to
> dust in his mouth, as it is written: 'Dust is the serpent's food' (Is 65,
> 25). These people however ate the manna which changed into many
> tastes, as it says: 'He gave them their requests' (Ps 106, 15), their
> desires were fulfilled, and as it says: 'These 40 years the Lord your
> God has been with you; you have lacked nothing' (Dt. 2, 7). Let the
> serpent, who eats many kinds of food and has but one taste in his
> mouth, come and punish those who eat one kind of food and
> experience the taste of many."

The introductory statement of this passage derives from the comment
of R. Ammi and R. Assi (Babylonian Amoraim of the 3rd-4th c.) on Is

---

*See, all sons of men, and take heed and listen, all sons of flesh! I cursed the serpent from
the beginning, and said to it: Dust shall be your food. And it did not murmur about the
food. I brought up my people free men from out of Egypt, and I made manna come down
for them from heaven, and I had quail pass by for them from the sea, and I made the well
come up for them from the deep. My people continue to murmur before me because of the
manna saying: We loathe this bread which is light food. Therefore let the serpent which
has not murmured about its food come forth and bite this people which murmurs about
their food. So the word of YHWH let loose fiery serpents among the people, which
bit the people and a great crowd from among Israel died. TJII Ginsburger 54
has the same text as TJII.*

[1]) Cf. 49, n. 2 above.

[2]) חקת 19 (ed. Zundel, 81); as Ginzberg, *The Legends of the Jews*, VI, 115, n. 653
indicates, Tanḥuma B. IV, 126 and Numbers R. 19, 22 (Slotki, II, 771) have the
same text. Considering that Midrash Tanḥuma was compiled in the 10th century,
while Numbers R. was compiled in the 12th century, the Numbers R. text most
probably derives from Midrash Tanḥuma; for the dates of compilation of these
haggadic collections, cf. Lehmann, "Aggadah," *art. cit.*, 216-217.

65, 25.[1]) The rest of the passage is homiletic application to our incident in Nb. The purpose of the passage is to explain why the Israelites were punished with serpents, and the main reason given here is an application of the lex talionis on the basis of the variegated taste of the manna for Israel and the uniform taste of the snake.

Since the Tanhuma passage and the PT text under consideration are commenting on the same verse of Nb, they naturally have some points in common — the serpent, the manna, and also the quote from Is 65, 25. However the differences between these haggadoth are far greater than the similarities. First of all, the literary form of PT Nb 11, 6 is that of the classical *rîb* pattern, so common in O.T. prophetic literature; the purpose of a *rîb* is to prove the innocence of the accused party, here God. Secondly, the quote from Is 65, 25 is related to Gen 3, 14 and the serpent of the Garden of Eden. Then the Bath Qol [2]) and the mention of the Exodus and the food-drink wonders of the wilderness all serve to underline the distinctiveness of the PT passage. Finally the focus of attention in PT is the murmuring motif, not the taste of manna. And its aim seems to be to prove that God is innocent of any covenant infraction and the people guilty; hence God's punishment for Israel's murmuring is a just one.[3]) All these characteristics of the PT passage indicate that it is not dependent upon nor does it derive from the Tanhuma text. Moreover, in the post-mishnaic rabbinic literature that considers this incident of Nb 21, 6, the main motive for the serpent's punishment here is slander, not murmuring; [4]) as the serpent of Gen 3 was punished for slandering, so also the people who slander God here are punished with serpents.

---

[1]) Yoma 75a (Jung, 360).

[2]) The mention of the Bath Qol cannot, unfortunately, be used to date a non-halakic midrash, cf. A. Guttmann, "The Significance of Miracles for Talmudic Judaism," *HUCA* 20 (1947), 363-406; Billerbeck, *Kommentar etc.*, I, 126 says relative to the Bath Qol here: "Diese Ausdrucksweise wird mit dem Streben zusammenhängen, das böse Verhängnis von Nu 21, 6 nicht auf Gott zurückzuführen," and to bolster this observation, cites Tg Lam 3, 38, which states that misfortune proceeds not from God's mouth, but from the Bath Qol; only good comes from God's mouth. However the Bath Qol was used indiscriminately for announcing fortune and misfortune alike throughout rabbinic literature; cf. L. Blau, "Bat Kol," *The Jewish Encyclopedia* (New York, 1903), II, 588-592; and Marti and Beer *Abot (Väter)*, 163-164.

[3]) This purpose derives from the nature of the *rîb* pattern used here; cf. J. Vella, *La Giustizia forense di Dio* (Supplementi alla Rivista Biblica I; Brescia, 1964), 65-104.

[4]) For references, cf. Ginzberg, *The Legends of the Jews*, VI, 115, n. 654.

In conclusion then, it seems that PT Nb 21, 5-6 ought be dated to the time of origin of the PT.

Before bringing this sub-section to a close, we ought consider this incident of Nb 21, 5-6 as it is recalled in the capsule summary of the Israelitic wilderness period to be found in the expanded first verse of Dt 1 in all the Targums, TO included. [1]) The first verse of Dt 1 reads:

> "These are the words which Moses spoke to all Israel beyond the Jordan, in the desert, in the Arabah over against Suph, between Paran and Tophel, Laban, Hazeroth and Di-Zahab."

The Targums, in their turn, take up these place names and append to them or interlace them with reminiscences of the wilderness period: [2])

N	TJI
These are the words which Moses spoke to all the children of *Israel.* And he reproached them while they were situated *beyond the Jordan.* Answering, Moses said to them: Was not the Law given you, children of Israel, *in the desert*, on Mt. Sinai, and was it not explained to you *in the plains* of Moab? What miracles YHWH did for you, children of Israel! When you stood at the *Reed* Sea, the sea separated itself before you, and twelve paths were made, one for each tribe. You provoked him at the sea, and were rebellious at the Reed Sea. And because of the spies which you sent from the desert of *Paran* to ex-	*These are the words* of complaint *which Moses spoke to all Israel.* He assembled them to himself when they were *beyond the Jordan*, then answered and spoke to them: Was not the Law given to you *in the desert* in Mt. Sinai, and was it not explained to you in the plains (מישריא = Arabah, plain) of Moab? What miracles and prodigies did the Holy One, blessed be He, do for you from the time you crossed along the shore of the *Reed* Sea (ימא דסוף = Suph), for he made a pathway for each tribe. You in turn turned aside from his word and provoked him to anger in *Paran*, because of the word of the spies, and *accused*

---

[1]) Cf. below, and G. Vermes, "Haggadah in the Onkelos Targum," *Journal of Semitic Studies* 8 (1963), 167-168.

[2]) The following texts are translated from the sample copy of the projected *Biblia Polyglotta Matritensia*, Series IV, ed. A. Díez Macho (Madrid, 1965), 6-9; the words in parentheses under N are lacking in N and supplied from TJII. The italicized portions indicate the words found in the MT Dt 1, 1; for the Aramaic equivalents in all the PT, consult the TJI column.

plore the land of Canaan, (it was decreed concerning you that you would not enter the land of Israel). And because of the manna concerning which you said: Our soul is weary of this bread, because it is light food, (he let loose the serpents among you). And in *Hazeroth*, where your corpses fell because of the meat which you desired, and because of the calf which you made, YHWH determined in his word to destroy you. But because he remembered in your regard the covenant which he struck with your fathers, with Abraham, with Isaac and with Jacob, and the tent of meeting which you made in his name, and YHWH's ark of the covenant which you brought into it, which you covered with pure *gold*, he spoke by his word and forgave your sins.

טפלתון מילי) = Tophel) him falsely, and murmured about the manna which he sent down for you, *white* (חיוור = Laban, white) from heaven. You demanded meat in *Hazeroth*, and it was fitting that you be destroyed from the midst of the world. But because he remembered in your behalf the merit of your just fathers and the tent of meeting and the ark of the covenant and the holy vessels which you plated with pure gold, he forgave you for the sin of the golden calf (דהבא = Di-Zahab).

TO in turn offers a simple skeleton sketch of the foregoing PT:

"These are the words which Moses spoke to all Israel beyond the Jordan. He reproved them because they had sinned in the desert, and had angered (God) in the plain over against the Reed Sea; because they had scorned (Tophel) the manna at Paran, and had angered (God) in Hazeroth on account of meat and made the golden calf (Di-Zahab)."[1]

Vermes has observed: "It is not difficult to see how all this was constructed. Since the list of place-names conveyed nothing to anyone, targumic tradition discovered in them references to various

---

[1] Vermes, "Haggadah in the Onkelos Targum," *art. cit.*, 167-168, notes: "(Onkelos) borrows, as usual, and from the usual sources, but maintains withal its own individual approach. For instance, the Palestinian Targums see in the 'wilderness' the place where the Law was given to Israel; but for Onkelos it is the site of a transgression. This is one of the many differences of detail. A wider divergence is noticeable in the form of the Haggadah. Onkelos relates Moses' words to the Israelites in the shape of an indirect speech, whereas in the Palestinian Targums the Lawgiver himself addresses the people."

events which occured after the exodus from Egypt." [1]) This is
certainly true, but it is not the full reason for the aforecited targumic
exegesis. From tannaitic times, the incipit of Deuteronomy was
considered as introducing Moses' words of reproof.[2]) Once this was
granted, then both the understandable place-names as well as the
enigmatic ones were ingeniously interpreted, in line with the purpose
of the speech, as places where the wilderness generation provoked
God to anger.[3]) The place-names that proved enigmatic and meant
nothing to anyone were Tophel and Laban. Thus R. Simeon b.
Yoḥai [4]) (130-160 AD) explains: "I have made a study of all the places

---

[1]) *Ibid.*, 167.

[2]) Cf. Josephus, Ant. IV, 8, 194-195 (Niese, 202),where he interprets his previous
synopsis of Moses' opening Deuteronomy speech as a rebuke; Pseudo-Philo,
Ant. XIX, 1-5, especially 5 (cited from M. R. James, *The Biblical Antiquities of
Philo* (London, 1917), 127-128; this work was originally written in Hebrew,
in Palestine, shortly after the fall of Jersusalem; cf. L. Cohn, "An Apocryphal
Work Ascribed to Philo of Alexandria," *Jewish Quarterly Review* 10 (1898), 277-332)
another synopsis of the Deuteronomy speech, clearly a rebuke; Siphre Dt 1
(cited from M. Friedmann (ed.), *Sifré debé Rab: der älteste halachische und hagadische
Midrasch zu Numeri u. Deuteronomium* (Vienna, 1864), 64b); and Leqaḥ Ṭob
Dt 1, 1 (Ugolino, XVI, 791; in Ugolino, this work is called Pesiqta) where this
exegesis is recorded anonymously. It is equally anonymous in Aboth de Rabbi
Nathan א c. 34 (cited from J. Goldin, *The Fathers according to Rabbi Nathan* (Yale
Judaica Series X; New Haven, 1955), 136-137); in this source, an expanded
form of Dt 1, 1 not unlike that in the PT is used to comment on M. Aboth V, 4:
"With ten temptations did our fathers tempt the Holy One, blessed is he, in the
wilderness." The presentation in Aboth de Rabbi Nathan א seems to be a combination of previously existing elements; in the first place, there are not ten place-
names in Dt 1, 1, so three more are added from Dt 9, 22—yielding a total of
eleven; thus Di-Zahab is left out of the ten trials; further the interpretation of
Suph and Paran are dependent upon R. Judah b. Ilaʿi (cf. 73, n. 5 below); that of
Tophel and Di-Zahab on R. Simeon b. Yoḥai or a contemporary (cf n. 4 & 73 n. 7
below), while that of Hazeroth seems a confused reference to the Aramaic based
exegesis of PT (cf. p. 74 below; Goldin's note 7, p. 206 f. explains nothing).
Moreover, the only elements of exegesis held in common by Aboth de Rabbi
Nathan א and PT are the explanations of Suph, Paran, Tophel and Di-Zahab,
which most probably derive from the aforementioned Tannaim. Finally, the
second recension of this work in S. Schechter (ed.), *Aboth de Rabbi Nathan*
(Vienna, 1887) c. 34, lacks this expansion of Dt 1, 1 and simply reports the ten
temptations as evolved by R. Judah b. Ilaʿi (cf. 73 n. 5 below).

[3]) Cf. Rashi on Dt 1,1: "Because these are words of reproof and he is enumerat-
ing here all the places where they provoked God to anger, therefore he suppresses
all mention of the matters in which they sinned and refers to them only by a
mere allusion contained in the names of these places out of regard for Israel,"
cited from Rosenbaum and Silbermann, V, 2.

[4]) This ascription is that of R. Tobiah b. R. Eliezer, Leqaḥ Ṭob Dt 1,1 (Ugolino,
XVI, 789); his contemporary Rashi has a similar comment ascribed to R. Joḥanan,
probably the Palestinian Amora of the 2nd-3rd century: "We have gone through
the whole Bible and we have found no place the name of which is Tophel or

through which Israel marched in order to find out whether Israel broke camp at Tophel and Laban; and we found only the frivolous words (דברים של תפלות) [1]) which they uttered against the manna, because it was white (לבן)." While the PT expressly mention the desert and the plain as the places where the Law was given and explained respectively, they may be equally intimating Israel's misconduct either at these occasions or in these places, e.g. the incidents recorded in Nb 3, 4 and Nb 25, 1 ff.

Be that as it may, all the traditions related in the PT, except the Hazeroth incident, are witnessed to by pre-mishnaic personages — "words of complaint" related to Dt 1, 1 = Pseudo-Philo and Josephus; [2]) the Law given in Sinai and explained in the plains of Moab = R. Akiba, R. Simeon and their predecessors; [3]) the miracles at the sea with a pathway for each tribe = anonymous but pre-mishnaic; [4]) Paran and the spies = R. Judah b. Ila'i (130-160 AD); [5]) Tophel and Laban = R. Simeon b. Yohai (130-160 AD); [6]) and Di-Zahab = again R. Simeon b. Yohai. [7]) Naturally, this does not prove

---

Laban! But the meaning is that he reproved them because of the calumnious statements (תפלו) they had made regarding the manna which was white (לבן) in color" (on Dt 1, 1, *loc. cit.*). The second generation Tanna, R. Ishmael likewise says he could find no such places as Laban and Tophel, while his contemporary R. Jose makes a comment similar to that of R. Simeon b. Yohai's, in D. Hoffmann (ed.), *Midrasch Tannaim zum Deuteronomium* (Berlin, 1909), 2, ad verba. The comment is certainly pre-mishnaic.

[1]) Both טפל (cf. TJI Dt 1, 1 above) and תפל mean "to paste." The derivatives of the latter word are תפלה meaning "frivolity, trivialness, indecency"; and תפלות meaning "frivolity, trivialness, obscenity." Siphre Dt 1 (Friedmann, 65a) thus explains "between Tophel and Pharan": דברי תפלות שתפלו על המן, "the frivolous words which they pasted on the manna" literally. Thus the verbs and their derivatives have much of the connotation of the word "to smear" in American usage; cf. Jastrow, *A Dictionary of the Targumim etc.*, I, 547; II, 1686 f. ad verba; and Rosenbaum and Silbermann, *op. cit.*, IV, 191-192—notes to p. 56b; V, 183—notes to p. 2.

[2]) Cf. previous page, n. 2.

[3]) Cf. Sotah 37b, cited from A. Cohen, *Sotah*: in I. Epstein (ed.), *The Babylonian Talmud*: *Nashim III* (London, 1936), 170.

[4]) There is an anonymous text citing the ten miracles at the Red Sea, one being a path for each tribe, in Mekilta on 14, 16 (Horovitz, 100-101); such a list is presupposed as known by M. Aboth V, 4; cf. Israelstam, *Aboth*, 60; Marti and Beer, *Abot (Väter)*, 122.

[5]) 'Arakin 15a (Jung, 85-86); our ascription of this haggada to R. Judah b. Ila'i follows the indication given in the index volume of *The Babylonian Talmud*, compiled by J. Slotki.

[6]) Cf. previous page.

[7]) Siphre Dt 1 (Friedmann, 65a); cf. Berakoth 32a (Simon, 195) and Sanhedrin 102a cited from J. Schachter and H. Freedman, *Sanhedrin*: in *The Babylonian*

that PT Dt 1,1 is pre-mishnaic; but it does indicate that there is nothing in our passage that is not pre-mishnaic.

We might note, also, that N and TJII have a more or less identical text, and both differ somewhat from TJI. They lack the treatment of the enigmatic place-names Tophel and Laban, pointed out above, even though they mention the manna incident of Nb 21, 5-6 in a place parallel to TJI. Whether this means that N and TJII did not know of R. Simeon b. Yoḥai's exegesis, and hence antedate it, or not is rather impossible to say. The linking of the incident in Nb 21, 4-9 to the place name Hazeroth is proper to the PT. This bit of exegesis took place in the following manner. In the O.T., the demands for meat took place at Kibroth-hattavah (Nb 11, 34-35) and along the way to the Reed Sea, around (לסבב) the land of Edom. PT Nb 21, 4 translates לסבב with לאחזרא, and from there gets a Hebraized form חזרות that would equal MT's חצרות of Dt 1, 1. The PT actually have the MT form of the word.

While this exegesis of Dt 1, 1 is of interest from the viewpoint of haggadic tradition in the PT and for targumic exegesis, it has not much new to say about the manna. It simply retells what was already told in PT Nb 21,6; and like that passage, PT Dt 1, 1 probably also dates to the time of the origin of the PT.

4) *Dt* 8, 3.16

N	TJI
3. And he afflicted you [1]) and made you hunger and fed you the manna which you did not know and your fathers did not know, in order to make it known to you that (not on bread alone *does* the son of man live, but) [2]) on whatever proceeds from the mouth *of the decree of the word* of YHWH will the son of man live.	3. And he afflicted you and made you hunger and fed you the manna which you did not know and your fathers did not know in order to make you know that not on bread alone *does* the son of man live, but on all that *was created by the word* of YHWH *does* the son of man live.

Talmud: Nezikin III (London, 1935), 693, where a similar exposition of Di-Zahab is ascribed to the school of R. Jannai.

[1]) In N all the second person pronouns are in the plural; TJI adheres closely to the Hebrew text.

[2]) The words in parentheses are written in the margin, but by the same hand responsible for this portion of the manuscript, hence not a gloss, but an insertion of an omission in the text. TJII: that not on *manna* alone.

16. Who fed you manna in the desert which your fathers did not know in order to afflict you and in order to test you, to do good for you at the end *of days*.

16. Who fed you the manna in the desert which your fathers did not know in order to afflict you and test you, to do good for you in your end.

In their exegesis of v 3, the PT part company. TJI takes the MT phrase: "all that proceeds from the mouth of YHWH," to mean creation. With this version, the text merely belabors the obvious — man needs other things for life, and perhaps other foods, than bread alone. This version does not exclude "spiritual" things, like the Law, feasts, etc., but it does not specify either. Further, TJI renders MT's יחיה with the form חיי which may be the perfect, the participle or even the noun "life" in the construct.[1]) However all of these forms yield the same sense, except that they would exclude the modal nuance allowed for by MT's imperfect.

As for N's handling of v 3, it is possible that N really adds nothing to the MT since its "decree of the word of YHWH" may simply be a targumic method of dealing with an anthropomorphism. However N's version of MT's "whatever proceeds from the mouth etc." points in another direction. These are the various versions of the MT phrase:

MT:	כל־מוצא פי־יהוה
TJI:	כל מה דאתברי על מימרא דיי
TO:	כל אפקות מימרא מן קדם יוי
N:	כל מה דנפק מן פם גזירת ממריה דיי
LXX:	ἐπὶ παντὶ ῥήματι τῷ ἐκπορευομένῳ διὰ στόματος θεοῦ

The version offered by TO — literally: "all the production of the word from before YHWH," i.e. everything produced by the word of YHWH — means more or less the same thing as TJI's "all that was created by the word of YHWH." That TO might mean: "every utterance of the word of YHWH," is perhaps also possible, but seems improbable once the anthropomorphic "mouth" drops out.

As for the N version, the preposition מן adds a new nuance to the phrase. "To proceed from the mouth" is an idiom for "to pro-

---

[1]) The version in Walton's *Polyglotta*, IV, 332, has "vita" twice in this verse.

mise," both in Hebrew and in Aramaic.[1]) Further, גזירת מימר can translate the Hebrew דבר, in a context meaning word, not thing (cf. MT and Tg Esther 1, 12). Hence the N version may have various meanings: "whatever proceeds from the mouth of the decree of the word of YHWH"; "whatever is promised by the word of YHWH"; "whatever proceeds from (or is promised by) the covenant of YHWH." Whatever the specific nuance may be, the fact is N is closer to LXX than any of the other Targums. We might even say that with regard to Dt 8, 3, N and LXX evidence a common interpretation and virtually verbal agreement.[2]) The idea in both is that for life, man needs not only food, but obedience to God's covenant commandments; and this was the object-lesson inculcated by the manna feeding.[3])

TJII specifies that man does not live on manna alone. With this fragment, and presuming the rest of the verse to be the same as either of the PT, Dt 8, 3 no longer continues to be a principle valid for all times, but simply a witness to what Israel learned during and for the period of its wilderness wanderings.

As for v 16, TJI adheres closely to the MT. N, on the other hand, has a reading very similar to LXX, or better, LXX shares both the MT (TJI) and the N readings;

MT: באחריתך
TJI & TO: בסופך
N: בסוף יומייה
LXX: ἐπ᾽ ἐσχάτων τῶν ἡμερῶν σου [4])

Thus TJI and TO tell us (with MT) that the generation to which Moses was speaking was fed the manna as a test of affliction with a view to eventual prosperity; the fathers of this generation are simply excluded (cf. v 3), since at the time of the speech they are presumably dead. And the prosperity intended is certainly the Promised Land.

---

[1]) Cf. Nb 30, 3; 32, 24; Judg. 11, 36; Jer 44, 17 in MT and PT—Targum Jonathan.

[2]) L. H. Brockington, "Septuagint and Targum," *ZAW* 66 (1954), 85 cites TO Dt 8, 3 and LXX Dt 8, 3 as an instance of common interpretation and virtually verbal agreement; naturally he did not know of N at the time.

[3]) For a similar interpretation, cf. Wis 16, 26; J. Fichtner, *Weisheit Salomos* (Handbuch zum Alten Testament; Tübingen, 1938), 61 says this verse stands "in deutlicher Beziehung auf Dt 8, 3 LXX"; this is possible, but it is equally possible that Wis 16, 26, N and LXX all independently depend upon a common oral tradition relative to Dt 8, 3.

[4]) Codd. Alexandrinus and Ambrosianus have: ἐσχάτω σου, a literal version of the MT.

N, on the other hand, by-passes the idea of prosperity in the Promised Land and interprets the test of affliction involved with the manna feeding [1]) as administered with a view to prosperity at the end of days,[2]) probably the eschatological period. The LXX interpretation shows hesitation both in the version settled upon and in the manuscript tradition.[4]) As the text stands, the passage may be read either historically ("at the end of your days"), or with a certain eschatological connotation ("at your end of days," i.e. of Israel). This hesitation in LXX may derive from a tradition similar to the one preserved in N.

As for dating the traditions in PT, it seems that N certainly dates from a period in which the LXX interpretation was produced; while there is no question of identical phrasing, the similarities point to a common exegetical tradition. TJI's interpretation of v 3 is quite close to the MT as is TO's. It is certainly possible that both TJI and TO once contained traditions similar to N, but later expurgated because the N tradition was quoted *as Scripture* by Christians.[3]) Aside from such conjecture, no other dating for TJI seems possible.

5) *Josh* 5, 5 — 6, 1

Tg Jonathan	MS 607 (ENA 2576) [4])
5,5. Although all the people who came out were circumcised, yet all the people who were born in the wilderness on the way after	5,5. (Their children were the generation who) asked of Moses and did not re(ceive the manna), and they sought after melons and

---

[1]) Cf. TJI Dt 34, 6: "He (God) taught us to feed the poor in that he sent down bread from heaven for the children of Israel."

[2]) Cf. G. W. Buchanan, "Eschatology and the 'End of Days'," *Journal of Near Eastern Studies* 20 (1961), 188-193.

[3]) Cf. Mt 4, 4; aside from the absence of an article, the text is identical with LXX.

[4]) A manuscript of the Jewish Theological Seminary of New York, published by Díez Macho, "Un nuevo Targum a los Profetas," *Estudios Biblicos* 15 (1956), 293-295; we translate the fragment in full to allow for a comparison with Tg Jonathan, cited from A. Sperber, *The Bible in Aramaic* (Leiden, 1959), Vol. II. The fragment represents a Babylonian recension of a Palestinian Targum to the prophets, since substantially the same text is contained in MS. T.-S. B 13/2 of the Cambridge University Library, a Palestinian recension not available to me. The lacunae in our text, marked by parentheses, have been filled by Díez Macho, presumably from the Palestinian recension which was available to him. Both fragments represent haphtaroth for the first day of the Passover, preserved as liturgical pieces; for a description, evaluation, etc. of this fragment, see Díez Macho, *art. cit.*, 287-292.

Tg Jonathan	MS 607 (ENA 2576)
their coming out of Egypt had not been circumcised.	cucumbers and leaks and onions and garlic. Then there was anger against them from before YHWH and he destroyed some of them with fire, and their fathers murmured against Moses in a fiery manner. And their children too gathered against Joshua; Joshua admonished them but they did not desist from their deeds in Egypt.
6. For the children of Israel walked 40 years in the wilderness till the whole *people* of warriors who came out of Egypt ended, because they did not heed the *word* of YHWH; for YHWH swore to them that they would not see the land which YHWH promised to their fathers to give us, a land *producing* milk and honey	6. For the children of Israel tarried 40 years because of the sins (of the spies); for Moses sent to (spy out the land . . .) and they produced a bad name (for the land) of Canaan. Then it was decreed against all the men (who believed them) (that they would not cross) the Jordan, but when (this) wicked (generation) would end, then their children would arise and would cross the Jordan, i.e. all the men (who came out) of Egypt (and who did not) heed the instruction of YHWH; against these YHWH swore that they would not see the land of Canaan which YHWH swore to their fathers, Abraham, Isaac and Jacob, to give them, a land which would not lack anything.
7. So it was their sons who *rose up* in their place that Joshua circumcised; for they were uncircumcised because they did not circumcise them on the way.	7. So it was the sons of those who rose up to subvert justice whom Joshua admonished, because they were stubborn for they did not heed the admonition on the way.

Tg Jonathan	MS 607 (ENA 2576)
8. Thus when all the *people* finished circumcising, they remained in their places in the camp until they were healed.	8. Then when all the generation which did not heed the admonition ceased, they returned to the Law of YHWH all the days of Joshua, as long as he lived.
9. Then YHWH said to Joshua: This day I have *removed* the shame of Egypt from over you. So the name of that place is called Gilgala to this day.	9. At that very time YHWH said to Joshua: This day I have removed the error of Egypt from among you. And so the name of that place is called Pasha until this day.
10. And the children of Israel encamped at Gilgala and held the Passover on the 14th day of the month in the evening on the plains of Jericho.	10. And the tribes that survived (of) the children of Israel from among the generation which died in the pestilence in the wilderness gathered themselves and held the Passover on the (four) teenth day of (Nisan when they encamped), and they did so at Jericho.
11. And they ate of the produce of the land from after the Passover, unleavened bread and parched grain, on that very day.	11. And (they encamped) and ate of the food of the land from after the feast day of the Passover, unleavened bread and parched grain, on that very day.
12. And the manna ceased on the day after it, when they ate of the produce of the land; and there was no longer manna for the children of Israel, and they ate of the produce of the land of Canaan in that year.	12. And the manna ceased from the day after they encamped, and they ate of the food of the land; and the manna did not come down any more for the children of Israel; they ate of the food which the land of Canaan produced in that year.
13. Now when Joshua was by Jericho, he raised his eyes and looked; and behold, a man standing before him with his drawn	13. Now when Joshua drew near to attack at Jericho, he lifted up his eyes and looked; and behold, an angel whose name was

Tg Jonathan	MS 607 (ENA 2576)
sword in his hand. Then Joshua went up to him and said to him: Did you *come to help* us or our enemies?	Uriel; his height (was about from) the earth to the heavens, and his breadth was about from Egypt to Jericho, and in his hand was his sword drawn clear of the sheath. Then Joshua fell upon his face to the ground and asked of him and said to him: Did you come to help us or do you seek to kill for our enemies?
14. And he said: No; for I, *an angel sent from before* YHWH, have come now.	14. (And he said to him:) I did not come to help and I am not for the enemies, but an angel sent from before YHWH. I come now to punish you because last evening you neglected the (daily burnt offering and) today you neglected (the study of the Torah). And he said: On account of which of (these then did you come?) And he said: I came on account of (the neglecting) of the Torah. And so Joshua fell upon his face upon the ground and said: Please do not forgive now the sins of your servant on account of his servants. And he said to him: Whatever is spoken from before YHWH against us must be accomplished and must be done.
15. Then *the angel sent from before* YHWH said to Joshua: Remove your shoes from your feet for the place where you stand is holy. And Joshua did so.	15. Then the angel sent from before YHWH said to Joshua: Let evil deeds pass away and convert and busy yourselves with the study of the Law [= Talmud] which you neglected. (This day) you are standing in order to ( )

Tg Jonathan   MS 607 (ENA 2576)

between yourselves the tables of
the covenant and its holy words.
And Joshua heeded in his soul
all that the angel sent from before
YHWH said to him and did so.

6,1. Now Jericho was closed   6,1. And the people of Jericho,
up and *surrounded* because of the   when they heard that the children
children of Israel; none *of them*   of Israel approached to make
went out and came in.   war against them, gathered to-
                                 gether . . . ¹)

The foregoing texts show that Tg Jonathan's version of Josh 5, 5—
6, 1 is in almost total conformity with MT, while the fragment in MS
607 goes its own way. The most notable overall differences between
the two is the total lack of mention of the circumcision episode in the
MS fragment as well as its repeated mention of the death of the wilderness generation (vv 6, 8, 10 and perhaps 9 also; against only v 6
in Tg Jonathan).²) As for Josh 5, 10-12, the Targums are more or
less the same as MT, except for the mention of the death of the wilderness generation in the MS fragment. No new light is thrown upon
the manna here,³) except that v 10 of the MS fragment intimates
that the manna ceased more or less with the extinction of the wilderness generation.

The MS fragment does contain some very old traditions. First
of all, its handling of v 9 resembles the method used by Josephus in
his exegesis of the place name Gilgal. Josephus ⁴) writes: "The place
where Joshua made camp was called Galgala; ⁵) this name means
freedom. For when they passed through (διαβάντες ⁶) the river, they
already realized that they were free from the hardship of the Egyp-

---

¹) The remainder of this ms contains only fragments of the rest of 6, 1-2.
²) Cf. Pseudo-Philo, Ant. XX, 3-6 (James, 133-134).
³) Nor in 5, 5 of the MS fragment; this passage is difficult to judge because
the verses preceding it are lacking. The incident mentioned in the first part of
v 5 may refer either to the Israelites while still in Egypt (Moses refused to give
them manna there) or to the incident in Nb 21, 4 ff.
⁴) Ant. V, 1, 34 (Niese, 231).
⁵) Cf. Tg Jonathan Josh 5, 9.10; an Aramaic form.
⁶) Philo, De Specialibus Legibus II, 2, 41; 18, 145.147, calls the Passover,
διαβατήρια; cited from L. Cohn, *Philonis Alexandrini Opera* (editio minor; Berlin,
1906), V, 82 & 103. Josephus, Ant. II, 14, 313 (Niese, 110) calls it ὑπερβάσια.

tians and that in the desert." The exegesis in the MS fragment seems to derive from a play on words involving v 8. Verse 8 tells us that when all the disobedient generation ceased (פסקו), then the people returned to the Law of YHWH; v 9 adds that at that very time, YHWH tells Joshua that on that day he has removed the error of Egypt, i.e. the disobedient generation. Hence the place is called פסחא. Thus while Josephus derives his exegesis from the idea that crossing the Jordan meant freedom from hardship, the MS fragment derives it from a word play offered by the information that at that time the disobedient wilderness generation ceased. We might note here that Josephus, like the MS fragment, makes no mention of the circumcision episode at Gilgal.[1]

The MS fragment v 13 informs us that the angel who appeared to Joshua was Uriel. This is a tradition proper to the fragment, since in rabbinic tradition the angel was Michael or Metatron.[2] While Uriel is known from pre-mishnaic times,[3] the mention of him in the fragment does not seem to offer a basis for dating this tradition.[4]

Then the exegesis presented in the first half of v 14 of the MS fragment is certainly pre-mishnaic. It is presupposed as known by Rab [5] (Babylonian Amora of the 2nd-3rd century) and R. Johanan [6] (Palestinian Amora of the 2nd-3rd century). As a matter of fact, this

---

[1]) Ginzberg, *The Legends of the Jews*, VI, 172, n. 16 cites Midrash Aggada Gen 17, 8 which reads: "Israel would never have been able to enter the Holy Land had not Joshua circumcised those born in the wilderness, since this land was promised the Patriarchs on condition that their descendants would observe the rite of circumcision." He then notes: "The statement of Josephus Ant V, 1, 11 that Gilgal means liberty is a haggadic rendering of Josh 5, 9 and perhaps presupposes the view quoted above that by performing the rite of circumcision at that place they definitely won their liberty." However Josephus does not mention the rite of circumcision at that place; neither does Pseudo-Philo, Ant. XX, 1-8 (James, 133-134).

[2]) Ginzberg, *The Legends of the Jews*, VI, 173, n. 21.

[3]) Cf. I Enoch 9, 1; 10, 1; 27, 2; 33, 4 which are sections of this book known to the author of the Book of Jubilees; cf. Charles, *The Apocrypha and Pseudepigrapha of the O.T.*, I, 170; in Numbers R. 2, 10 (Slotki, 39) Uriel is listed along with Michael, Gabriel and Raphael just as in I Enoch 9, 1.

[4]) Interestingly enough, Uriel is not mentioned in the Babylonian Talmud, at least the name is not listed in the thorough index compiled by J. Slotki, *The Babylonian Talmud*, ed. I. Epstein.

[5]) 'Erubin 63b (Slotki, 444-445); *ibid.* there is the opinion of R. Abba b. Papa (Palestinian Amora of the 4th century) acccording to whom Joshua was punished for preventing Israel for one night from the duty of propagation; his argument is Josh 5, 13.

[6]) Megillah 3a (Simon, 12) and Sanhedrin 44a-b (Schachter and Freedman, 289-290).

verse may be the key to dating the traditions contained in this fragment. To begin with, Josh 5 was certainly a Passover haphtarah; in
this capacity, its high antiquity is intimated by the fact that in the
Babylonian Talmud [1]) the halaka directing its usage at Passover is
anonymous.[2]) Further, this usage of Josh 5 as Passover haphtarah
is of Palestinian origin since the Babylonian rabbis followed Palestinian festival usages.[3]) Now haphtaroth, though perhaps not fixed
by calendar, were in use in the first half of the first century (cf. Lk
4, 16; Acts 13, 15; 15, 21). Büchler[4]) has suggested that the earliest
haphtaroth ought be sought in those passages of the prophets used
in the controversy of the Pharisees and Sadducees concerning the
festivals and the Temple worship. And our MS fragment vv 14-15
probably echoes the Pharisee-Sadducee dispute over payment for
the daily burnt offering (= Tamid).[5]) In this perspective, v 14 would
mean: For an individual the study of the Law is more important
than the daily burnt offering, which is to be paid for by all the people.[6])
This interpretation of MS fragment v 14 might also shed light on
the obscure penultimate sentence of the same verse. Granting the
ancient tradition that Joshua was punished for something, this
sentence might mean: Please do not forgive now the sins of your
servant (i.e. Joshua) on account of his servants (i.e. those in charge
of the Tamid offering, the Sadducees in control of the Temple).

An interpretation of this sort is further bolstered by v 15 in the
MS fragment. This verse underlines the obligation of the individual
to convert and to study the Law. In a parallel tradition interpreting
v 15, preserved in Seder Eliahu R. 18 [7]) Joshua is berated for not

---

[1]) Megillah 31a (Simon, 187).

[2]) Cf. 52, n. 31 above; such anonymous halaka have a good probability
in their favor of dating from the time of the Temple.

[3]) Cf. A. Büchler, "The Reading of the Law and the Prophets in a Triennial
Cycle II," *Jewish Quarterly Review* 6 (1894), 17-18.

[4]) *Ibid.*, 6.

[5]) Cf. J. Rabbinowitz, *Mishnah Megillah* (London, 1931), 98; the Pharisees
maintained public money (i.e. from the Temple treasury) was to be used to pay
for the Tamid; the Sadducees said the cost might be defrayed by a private individual. The Pharisees won the dispute in 79 BC.

[6]) Naturally, this verse might simply wish to inculcate the higher value of
studying the Law over offering sacrifices, especially after the destruction of the
Temple. Yet cf. the curious remark of R. Samuel b. Unia (Babylonian Amora)
in Megillah 3b (Simon, 12): "The study of the Torah is greater than the offering
of daily sacrifices, as it says: 'I have come now' (Josh 5, 14)—There is no contradiction: in one case (the study) of an individual is meant, in the other (the Tamid?)
that of the whole people."

[7]) L. M. Friedmann (ed.), *Seder Eliahu rabba und Seder Eliahu zuta* (Vienna,

taking off his shoes, i.e. for not mourning over the neglect of the
Torah and the cessation of the manna. Our MS fragment does not
even mention the removal of shoes indicated in the MT. Rather the
point of the MS fragment is a reproof to Joshua and Israel for not
studying the Law. However if the word for the study of the Law
(תלמודה) be a reference to the rabbinic corpus, the Talmud, then obviously the MS fragment would be a very late creation. On the other
hand, there is no indication that this is the meaning of the word here.

In short, there is nothing in the fragment to indicate that its
traditions do not date from pre-mishnaic times. And if vv 14-15
mirror the Tamid dispute, the traditions in this MS fragment could
be pre-Christian. However the traditions of this Passover haphtarah
cannot be positively dated either.

6) *Pss* 78, 23-25; 105, 40-42

The extant Targum on the Psalms is of Palestinian origin, even
though reworked and touched up by later hands.[1]) And therefore this
Targum ought be considered in any treatment of the exegetical traditions of the PT. We shall first consider Tg Ps 78, 23-25:

v 23: He commanded the clouds above,
      and opened the gates of heaven.

v 24: And *he sent down* upon them manna to eat,
      and he gave them heavenly grain.

v 25: *Sons of men* ate *food which came down from the dwelling* of angels,
      he sent them foodstuff to the full.

There are two items of interpretation in this passage. The first
comes in v 24, where the MT's "to rain" is rendered "to send down."
As indicated above,[2]) this way of speaking of the giving of the manna
is typical of the PT as well as of rabbinic literature with reference to
Ex 16, 4.

1902), 101-102; the text reads: "An angel went forth to destroy the whole world;
he said: The manna has ceased and the Torah has been neglected, as it says:
'and the captain of the Lord's army etc.' (Josh 5, 15). He said to him: What then
Joshua, why do you have your shoes on and why are you not mourning over
Israel for whom the manna has ceased and the Law neglected? Take off your
shoes!" Cf. the use of the word בטל, "to cease, neglect," 4 times in this Hebrew
passage and 4 times in vv 14-15 of our Aramaic fragment; note also no mention
of the Tamid here. In his introduction, Friedmann dates the Seder Eliahu R.
in general to the time of R. Anan, a Babylonian Amora of the 3rd century.
   [1]) Cf. Le Déaut, *Introduction à la littérature targumique*, I, 132-135.
   [2]) P. 54.

The other interpretation comes in v 25. MT tells us: "Man ate the bread of the powerful beings." LXX, in turn, explicitly identifies these powerful beings as ἄγγελοι, hence translates: "Man ate bread of angels," an interpretation developed at some length in Wis 16, 20 ff. This exegetical tradition was not entirely alien to Palestine, since Pseudo-Philo records it: "But know that you ate the bread of angels forty years." [1]) Tg Psalms on the other hand offers an interpretation which became the rabbinic standard after Akiba. The Babylonian Talmud reports that Akiba, like Pseudo-Philo, held that the manna was the food of angels.[2]) But his contemporary, R. Ishmael (both died ca. 135 AD) held that angels neither ate nor drank, citing Dt 9, 18 as proof. After this discussion, rabbinic tradition consistently interprets אבירים as not referring directly to angels.[3]) Hence the interpretation offered in Tg Ps 78, 25 dates to after Akiba.

As for Tg Ps 105, 40-42, the text is identical with MT except for v 40:

They asked *for meat*, and he brought quail,
and sated them with bread from heaven.

Thus Tg Ps 105 specifies what was asked for, while MT and LXX do not. But like LXX, our passage reads: "*they* asked" = ᾔτησαν, either because this was the reading of the Hebrew text it translated, or because it wishes to refer the asking to the sons of Israel — for which they were punished.

These are all the passages in the PT, to our knowledge, which speak of the manna in the same texts or contexts as does the MT. However the PT also offer other haggadic elements relative to the manna in rather varied contexts. We shall now turn to consider these elements.

---

[1]) Pseudo-Philo, Ant. XIX, 6 (James, 128).

[2]) Yoma 75b (Jung, 367).

[3]) The general interpretation in rabbinic sources is that אבירים refers to the members of the body, the manna being directly absorbed without undergoing the usual metabolic processes—cf. R. Ishmael's opinion in Yoma 75b (Jung, 367); also Mekilta on 16, 15 (Horovitz, 167) and Midrash on Ps 78, 4 (Braude, II, 23-24). Other opinions cited in the foregoing sources: the manna fell on the members, i.e. arms and hands, and was directly eaten, thus Mekilta, *loc. cit.*; cf. Josephus Ant. III, 1, 26 (Niese, 122); "food of angels" meant the Israelites became mighty as angels by eating the manna, thus Midrash on Ps 78, 4 *loc. cit.*; cf. the sources and discussion in Ginzberg, *The Legends of the Jews*, V, 236, n. 143.

B. Further Mention of the Manna in the Palestinian Targums

Aside from cursory mention of the manna in the course of the Pentateuch narrative (e.g. TJI Ex 18, 9), the PT offer two other passages worth consideration.[1]) These are Tg Eccles 12, 11 and Tg Cant 4, 5.

1) *Tg Eccles* 12, 11

MT	Tg
11. The sayings of the wise are like goads, and like nails firmly fastened are the collected sayings which are given by one shepherd.	11. The sayings of the wise are like goads and prods which impel those in need of knowledge to learn knowledge, like the goad teaches the ox; and the rabbis of the Sanhedrin are the masters of the halakoth and midrashim, which were given through Moses the prophet, who alone fed (like a shepherd: רעא) the people of the house of Israel in the desert with manna and desirable things.

The exegetical traditions clustered together in this verse of the Targum are of uneven age, but all would apparently antedate the Jerusalem Talmud. That the goads refer to impelling a person to learning and knowledge is an anonymous tradition preserved in the Jerusalem Talmud.[2]) Further, the targumic verse under consideration omits an interpretation of the phrase "like nails firmly fastened,"[3])

---

[1]) On the Palestinian origin of the Targums considered here, cf. Le Déaut, *Introduction à la littérature targumique*, I, 138-144. Tg Jonathan has a reference to manna in Ez 16, 13: "I fed you manna which was good like sifted fine flour and like honey and like oil." This interpretation derives from v 19 of the same chapter, where these things are sacrificed to the golden calf according to the exegesis of the Amoraim, and considered to be simply the manna, cf. Midrash on Ps 3, 3 (Braude, I, 54-55); R. Bloch, "Ézéchiel XVI: exemple parfait du procédé midrashique dans la Bible," *Cahiers Sioniens* 9 (1955), 193-223, especially 217-219.

[2]) J. Sanhedrin X, 1 (Schwab, XI, 43); the same tradition is also reported anonymously in Eccles R. XII, 11, par. 1 cited from A. Cohen, *Ecclesiastes*: in H. Freedmon and M. Simon (eds.), *Midrash Rabbah* (London, 1939), VIII, 312; however in Numbers R. 14, 4 (Slotki, 577) it is ascribed to a certain R. Nathan; but there are too many R. Nathan's in rabbinic literature to allow for determining who this particular R. Nathan might be.

[3]) Unless the phrase, "the rabbis of the Sanhedrin," refers to this phrase.

and instead offers two traditions on the meaning of בעלי אספות (collected sayings). This phrase is interpreted as referring to the Sanhedrin in the Jerusalem Talmud.[1]) On the other hand, the interpretation "masters of the halakoth and midrashim" seems to derive from
the oldest datable comment on this verse, that of R. Eleazar b.
Azariah (Tanna of the 1st-2nd century).[2]) Finally, the Targum specifies that the halakoth and midrashim were given *through* Moses the
prophet who alone shepherded the people of Israel. This item is
meant as an interpretation of the phrase "given by one shepherd" in
the MT; and this interpretation derives from early tannaitic times,
although the earliest datable sources do not specify Moses by name.[3])
As for the final portion of this verse, namely that Moses the prophet
alone fed Israel like a shepherd [4]) in the wilderness with manna and
other desirable things, this phrase too is an interpretation of "one
shepherd": דרעא בלחודוי = רעה אחד.

The tradition of Moses as shepherd of Israel can be dated to the
1st century AD.[5]) Now if the verb רעא in our verse be taken in the
sense that Moses simply shepherded Israel and led the people to the
manna provided so wonderfully by YHWH, then this interpretation
would date to the origins of the tradition of Moses as shepherd of
Israel. But if that verb be taken in the sense that Moses himself fed
the people, that he provided the manna for them, then the tradition
would date to the 3rd-4th century. The originator of this latter
tradition according to which Moses was the author of the wondrous
deeds of the Exodus and the desert period seems to be Rabbah
(Babylonian Amora of the 3rd-4th century).[6]) The idea that Moses

---

[1]) Anonymously in J. Sanhedrin X, 1 (Schwab, XI, 44) as well as Numbers
R. 14, 4 (Slotki, 582); Eccles. R. XII, 11, par. 1 (Cohen, 313) and Siphre Dt 41
(Friedmann, 80a).

[2]) Ḥagigah 3a-b (Abrahams, 10); and the parallel passage in Tosephta Soṭah
VII, 9-12 (Zuckermandel, 307).

[3]) Numbers R. 14, 4 (Slotki, 578) has R. Simeon b. Halafta (Tanna of the
2nd century) relating this exegesis in the name of R. Aḥa; Ḥagigah 3b (Abrahams,
10) has the following: "One God gave them (halakoth); one leader uttered them
from the mouth of the Lord of all creation"; the parallel in Tosephta Soṭah
VII, 12 (Zuckermandel, 307) has the comment: "one shepherd received them
(halakoth), one God created them." In all these passages the shepherd is naturally
Moses; cf. M. Aboth I, 1 (Marti and Beer, 2).

[4]) On Moses as shepherd in rabbinic tradition, cf. R. Bloch, "Quelques aspects
de la figure de Moïse dans la tradition rabbinique," *art. cit.*, 138-139; as regards
Moses the prophet, cf. *ibid.*, 138, n. 127: the rabbinic tradition, like the biblical,
does not develop this theme.

[5]) Cf. Pseudo-Philo, Ant. XIX, 3 (James, 127).

[6]) Soṭah 35a (Cohen, 171); the same tradition is repeated anonymously in

had the manna fall is often linked up with the equally late idea
that the last redeemer would be like the first redeemer, Moses; [1])
this latter idea is the formulation of R. Levi (Babylonian Amora of
the 3rd century). [2])

Thus while the traditions in Tg Eccles 12, 11 all antedate the
Jerusalem Talmud, they cannot be uniformly dated otherwise. With
regard to the tradition of Moses leading the people like a shepherd
to the manna, this tradition would be of the first century. But if the
text be taken as indicating that Moses himself made the manna come
down tor the people, then the tradition would be very late.[3])

2) *Tg Cant* 4, 5

MT	Tg
4,5. Your two breasts are like two fawns, twins of a gazelle, that feed among the lilies.	4,5. Your two liberators, who are going to liberate you, the Messiah son of David and the Messiah son of Ephraim are like Moses and Aaron, the sons of

---

Siphre Dt 339 (Friedmann, 141b) and Petirat Moshe; cf. Ginzberg, *The Legends
of the Jews*, VI, 149, n. 892; 151, n. 904.

[1]) Eccles. R. I, 9, par. 1 (Cohen, 33); Numbers R. 11, 2 (Slotki, 413); and cf.
the parallels cited by Billerbeck, *Kommentar*, II, 481.

[2]) Cf. I. Sonne, "The Paintings of the Dura Synagogue," *HUCA* 20 (1947),
382 and n. 97.

[3]) However cf. Jn 6, 32: "It was not Moses who gave you bread from
heaven..." This seems to presuppose that Jesus' audience (or John's readers)
held that Moses gave the manna; and this tradition is also preserved by Irenaeus
(d. 202): "Moses gave the fathers manna as food," *Fragment* 19 (PG VII, 1241);
and especially by Aphraates (d. 350) in his *Demonstrationes* (R. Graffin (ed.),
Patrologia Syriaca (Paris, 1894) I, 33, 152, 960), where Moses performs the Exodus
and wilderness miracles through faith and prayer. Further, if Jn 6, 32 be read
as an תקרי אל verse as suggested by P. Borgen, *Bread from Heaven*, 61 ff., then
the tradition that Moses was directly responsible for the manna would a fortiori
belong to the first century. In fact it seems that this tradition was purposefully
suppressed by rabbinic Judaism in the first century, only to emerge again in the
3rd-4th century. The cause of this suppression seems to have been a reaction
against the deification of the Messiah ushered in by Christianity; the Moses—
Jesus—Messiah parallelism was to be rendered impotent by ascribing the Exodus
and wilderness wonders to God himself and God alone; cf. D. Daube, "The
Earliest Structure of the Gospels," *NTS* 5 (1958/1959), 177-178 and notes.
Note also that even the Samaritan Memar Marqah, while extolling Moses the
prophet, generally ascribes the wilderness wonders directly to God; cf. Mac-
Donald, *Memar Marqah: the Teaching of Marqah*, II, on the manna directly from
God: 39, 164, 172, 223; but Moses' prayers brought the manna: 207; and Moses
acted as intermediary: 223.

MT   Tg

Jochebed, who are like twins of a
gazelle, who fed (like shepherds)
the people of the house of Israel,
through their merits, during 40
years in the wilderness, with the
manna, the fat birds and the
water of Miriam's well.

In a more or less parallel passage, Cant 7, 4 (E.VV. 7, 3), the Targum
repeats the foregoing exegetical traditions in part:

MT   Tg

7,4. Your two breasts are like   7,4. Your two liberators, who
two fawns, twins of a gazelle.   are going to liberate you, the
                                        Messiah son of David and the
                                        Messiah son of Ephraim, are
                                        like Moses and Aaron, the sons
                                        of Jochebed, who are like twins
                                        of a gazelle.

Thus in the exegesis offered in the Targum, "two breasts" = two
liberators; "two fawns" = Moses and Aaron; while the twins that
feed (הרועים) in Cant 4, 5 are interpreted as Moses and Aaron who
(transitively) feed the people like shepherds (רעו). The elements
for such an exegesis were present in rabbinic tradition from pre-
mishnaic times. However the form in which this exegesis is presented
in the Targum here is quite distinctive.

In the first place, the "two breasts" of Cant 4, 5 and 7, 4 are interpreted of Moses and Aaron in Canticles R. IV, 5, par. 1.[1]) Then,
while the tannaitic rabbis know of an Ephraimitic Messiah, the earliest sources always call him the Messiah son of Joseph. [2]) Hence
the exegesis in the first part of Tg Cant 4, 5 probably dates to a late
period, when the title "Messiah son of Ephraim" came into use,[3])

---

[1]) M. Simon, *Song of Songs*: in H. Freedman and M. Simon (eds.), *Midrash
Rabbah* (London, 1939), IX, 198, anonymously cited.

[2]) Sukkah 52a (Slotki, 246), cites R. Dosa, a 2nd century Tanna; Sukkah 52b
(Slotki, 251) cites R. Hana b. Bizna citing R. Simeon Hasida, also a 2nd century
Tanna.

[3]) The notion of an Ephraimitic Messiah probably dates from ca. 135 AD,

and when the exegesis of "two breasts" was referred to the two Messiahs instead of to Moses and Aaron.

As for the final exegetical tradition in our verse, that Moses and Aaron were responsible for the manna, the fat birds (quail) and Miriam's well, this too is a very ancient piece of haggada. But again, the traditional haggada telling of the manna, cloud, and well due to the merits of Moses, Aaron and Miriam respectively, is a bit forced here to fit the context of Cant 4, 5 which speaks of only two fawns. The oldest datable form of this tradition would be Pseudo-Philo, who records:

> "These are the three things which God gave his people for the sake of three persons, that is the well of the water of Mara for Maria's sake and the pillar of cloud for Aaron's sake, and the manna for the sake of Moses. And when these three came to an end, those three gifts were taken away from them." [1]

This tradition is often repeated in rabbinic literature, substantially the same, though with slight variations; yet in none of the oldest versions are the quail related to Aaron's merits. Rather, Aaron is always linked up with the cloud of glory.[2] Moreover, it is possible that the targumist is intimating that the Israelites of the wilderness wanderings had a ready supply of quail so long as Aaron was alive.

Be that as it may, our targumic verse likewise further intimates a relationship between the Messiahs and the wilderness wonders by comparing these Messiahs with Moses and Aaron. This relationship, too, is an ancient one. But as in the previous bits of exegetical tradition, the targumist offers a distinctive presentation, undoubtedly because of his own contemporary problems and the accumulation of various traditions at the date when he recorded his exegesis.

---

certainly not sooner; cf. H. H. Rowley, "The Suffering Servant and the Davidic Messiah," *Oudtestamentische Studiën* 8 (1950), 100-136; on the Targum, 107, n. 29.

[1]) Ant. XX, 8 (James, 134-135); Josephus, Ant. III, 1, 31 (Niese, 123) also tells us the Israelites were given the manna by God as a favor to Moses: Μωυσεῖ χαριζόμενον.

[2]) E.g. Mekilta on 16, 35 (Horovitz, 173) R. Joshua, ca. 90 AD; Ta'anith 9a (Rabbinowitz, 38) R. Jose b. Judah, 2nd century; Tosephta Soṭah II, 10 (Zuckermandel, 315-316) also R. Jose b. Judah; Numbers R. 1, 2 (Slotki, 3) anonymous; Numbers R. 1, 2 (Slotki, 4) R. Berekiah in the name of R. Levi, 3rd century; Numbers R. 13, 2 (Slotki, 553); Leviticus R. 27, 6 (Israelstam and Slotki, 350) R. Berekiah; Canticles R. IV, 5, par. 2 (Simon, 200) R. Jose; Eccles R. VII, 1, par. 4 (Cohen, 171) anonymous; cf. also R. Le Déaut, "Miryam, soeur de Moïse, et Marie, mère du Messie," *Biblica* 45 (1964), 209-213; and the comparison in Cohn, "An Apocryphal Work Ascribed to Philo of Alexandria," *art. cit.*, 321.

An early form of the tradition linking a single Messiah with the miraculous wilderness feedings is to be found in the Syriac Apocalypse of Baruch (100-130 AD)[1] The text in question is II Baruch 29, 6-8:

v 6: And those who hunger shall rejoice and they
shall again see wondrous deeds every day.
v 7: For spirits shall go out from before me
in order to fetch, every morning, the odor of
aromatic fruit, and at the close of day,
clouds showering forth dew of health.
v 8: And it shall be in those days, that the treasury of manna
shall once again descend from on high,
and they shall eat of it in those years, for
these are they who have come to the end of time.[2]

It would seem that our targumist took a tradition similar to the one in II Baruch and applied it to the two Messiahs idea current in his day. Consequently, while Tg Cant 4, 5 echoes many ancient exegetical traditions, in its extant form it is of late origin.

C. CONCLUSION

From the foregoing considerations of the manna tradition as developed and preserved in the Palestinian Targums, we might draw the following conclusions:

1) *As to date*

The PT to the Pentateuch all contain ancient traditions, most of which are pre-mishnaic. The traditions in PT Ex 16 and PT Dt 8, 3.16 can, by and large, be dated to N.T. times; the traditions in PT Nb 11, 6-9 and 21, 5-6 certainly date to the origins of the PT. On the other hand, Tg Ps 78, 23-25, while pre-mishnaic, does not date to

---

[1]) Cf. O. Eissfeldt, *The Old Testament: an Introduction*, trans. P. Ackroyd (London, 1965), 629-630; this work as a whole is dependent upon Pseudo-Philo, cf. Cohn, "An Apocryphal Work Ascribed to Philo of Alexandria," *art. cit.*, 277-332.

[2]) Text from M. Kmosko (ed.), *Liber Apocrypseos Baruch Filii Neriae*: in R. Graffin (ed.), *Patrologia Syriaca* (Paris, 1907), II, 1115-1116; this passage is reminiscent of Neh 9, 20 and is probably an expansion of it; it also recalls Josephus, Ant. III, 1, 27 (Niese, 122): what fell from heaven was not δρόσος ἀλλ' ἐπὶ σωτηρία τῇ αὐτῶν; and TJI Ex 16, 4.15. C. C. Torrey, "The Messiah Son of Ephraim," *JBL* 66 (1947), 263-266 relates this passage to the Messiah ben Ephraim, but this position is amply refuted by Rowley, "The Suffering Servant etc.," *art. cit., passim.*

N.T. times, and Tg Cant 4, 5 and Tg Eccles 12, 11 are certainly postmishnaic. As for Tg MS fragment Josh 5, 5 ff., it cannot be certainly dated as post-mishnaic; rather it may be pre-mishnaic, even contemporary with N.T. times, although there is nothing to prove this with certainty

2) *As to exegetical traditions*

(a) PT Ex 16 for the most part simply render explicitly what is already implicit in the MT and update the passage for it to have a contemporary message for its hearers. Thus:

v 1   specifies the month in terms of the calendar in use at the time;
v 2   explains precisely why the Israelites began to murmur — their food ran out;
v 4   introduces the current way of speaking about the manna; it is "sent down, made to come down," not "rained down"; further, the word "heaven" permits TJI to tell of the origin of the manna, which was hidden away or reserved for the Israelites from the beginning;
v 5   tells of contemporary Sabbath practice relative to food;
v 13 allows for the exegesis of אגוחתא, (dew-)fall as table or platter, since this Aramaic word can mean both;
v 15 is a repeat of the phrase of v 4;
v 21 contains contemporary exegesis of the phrase "morning by morning" as applied in halaka, while the mention of the manna's melting allows for an explanation of what happened to the melted manna;
v 23 explains clearly how Sabbath cooking is to take place;
v 29 relates contemporary Sabbath carrying and walking limits;
v 35 narrates precisely how long the Israelites had the manna.

The remaining items in these PT are simply the ordinary targumic traits, aside from the mention of Dathan and Abiram in TJI v 20, which seems to be a latter exegetical tradition regarding who precisely proved disobedient on this occasion.

(b) PT Nb 11, 6-9 and 21, 5-6 simply amplify the murmuring motif, already well connected with the manna in the O.T.; the former passage also offers some ancient speculation on the taste of the manna, a topic of divergent traditions already in the O.T.

(c) PT Dt 8, 3.16 further develop the "spiritualizing" of the manna, explicitly telling that the purpose of the manna was to be an object-lesson for total dependence on God (TJI), or more specifically, on God's word (N). Further, the purpose of the affliction involved with the manna feeding is eschatological good (N).

(d) Tg. Josh 5, 5 ff. in the MS fragment, a Palestinian Targum, is quite distinctive. Its omission of the mention of circumcision and its highlighting of the death of the wilderness generation are elements proper to it. On the other hand, Joshua's interview with the angel Uriel follows the lines of the contemporary rabbinic exegesis of the passages involved.

(e) Tg Ps 78, 23-25 brings the O.T. verse in line with current speculation on angels — they do not eat, hence manna is not the bread of angels, but bread from where angels live, i.e. heaven. Tg Ps 105, 40 adds nothing really new.

(f) Tg Eccles 12, 11 and Tg Cant 4, 5 both mention the manna mainly because of the presence of the root רעא in the O.T. texts. This root recalls the traditional exegesis of Zach 11, 8: "And I destroyed the three shepherds (הרעים) in one month," the three shepherds being Moses, Aaron and Miriam (פרנסים in Taʿanith 9a and Tosephta Soṭah II, 10; cf. 90, n. 2 above). While these last two Targums mirror an old tradition with regard to the manna, they apply the tradition to their own contemporary ends.

Thus by and large, the PT follow the lines already laid down in O.T. tradition. Their rendering explicit of what is implicit in the O.T. is simply a continuation of the midrashic procedure already at work and evidenced in the subsequent stages of the development of the manna tradition in the O.T. Palestinian books.

CHAPTER THREE

THE PALESTINIAN MANNA TRADITION AND THE NEW TESTAMENT

There are three significant mentions of the manna in the N.T.: 1 Cor 10, 3; Apoc 2, 17; Jn 6, 31 ff.[1]) In this section of our work, we propose to review these N.T. texts to see whether the manna tradition as handed down through the PT can shed any light on them.

1) 1 *Cor* 10, 3

Chapter 10 of the first epistle to the Corinthians begins with a midrash which, as Neuenzeit [2]) notes, does honor to Paul's rabbinic schooling:

v 1: For I should not like you to be ignorant of the fact, bretheren, that our fathers all were under the cloud, and all passed through the sea,

v 2: and all were baptized into Moses by means of the cloud and by means of the sea,

v 3: and all ate the same spiritual food,

v 4: and all drank the same spiritual drink, for they used to drink of the accompanying spiritual rock; the rock however was the Messiah.

v 5: But God was not pleased with most of them, for they were laid low in the wilderness.

In this passage, the spiritual food is obviously the manna. The problem, however, is why is it called spiritual. St. Paul felt a similar problem with calling the drink of the wilderness generation spiritual; the γάρ and consequent clarification of v 4b point to this. In brief, the problem is what is the meaning of the adjective πνευματικός in this passage. Exegetes agree that the attribute "spiritual" as employed here has the same meaning in all three instances; but they

---

[1]) For Heb. 9, 4, cf. 61 above.

[2]) P. Neuenzeit, *Das Herrenmahl*: *Studien zur paulinischen Eucharistieauffassung* (Studien zum A.T. und N.T. I; Munich, 1960), 45; it is beyond the scope of this study to enter upon a detailed exegesis of the context and text of this passage, for which cf. Neuenzeit, *ibid.*, 44 ff., and the references there as well as the commentaries cited below.

differ as to what precisely this meaning might be. Some hold "spiritual" here means "conveying pneuma" (Käsemann [1])); having "a spiritual meaning and influence . . . endowed for all with a 'spiritual' grace" (Findlay [2])); a "means of deification" (Mauser [3])); a combination of miraculous, plus the "spiritual" interpretation given to the manna and the well in the course of Israel's history, plus figurative — in relationship to the Eucharist (Martelet [4])). Others deem "spiritual" here means prophetic or figurative (Spicq [5])); miraculous as well as having a spiritual meaning (as sign of the body and blood of Christ), and this second sense being the formal one here (Allo [6])). Finally, there are those, possibly the majority, who claim that "spiritual" here means miraculous, supernatural (Lietzmann, Gutjahr, Sickenberger [7])); of supernatural origin (Robertson and Plummer [8])); of supernatural, divinely spiritual origin and essence (Heinrici [9])); not of the order of creation, but from God creatively at work in his Spirit (Bachmann [10])); deriving directly out of God's world and bestowing God's power (Schweizer, [11]) Neuenzeit [12])). Thus according to the foregoing opinions, "spiritual" here means (1) bestowing pneuma, or (2) figurative, prophetic, with a view to the Eucharist, or (3) of spiritual, heavenly, divine origin.

The first meaning, which Goppelt claims derives from current

---

[1]) E. Käsemann, "Anliegen und Eigenart der paulinischen Abendmahlslehre," *Evangelische Theologie* 7 (1947/1948): in *Essays on New Testament Themes*, trans. W. J. Montague (Studies in Biblical Theology 41; London, 1964), 113; similarly L. Goppelt, *TWNT*, VI, 147.

[2]) G. G. Findlay, *St. Paul's First Epistle to the Corinthians*: in W. R. Nicoll (ed.), *The Expositor's Greek Testament* (London, 1900), II, 858.

[3]) U. W. Mauser, *Christ in the Wilderness* (Studies in Biblical Theology 39; London, 1963), 64.

[4]) G. Martelet, "Sacrements, figures et exhortation en I Cor X, 1-11," *RSR* 44 (1956), 354 ff.

[5]) C. Spicq, *Épître aux Corinthiens* (La Sainte Bible, Pirot-Clamer; Paris, 1948), 237.

[6]) E. B. Allo, *Saint Paul: Première Épître aux Corinthiens* (EB; Paris, 1934), 230-231.

[7]) Cited by Allo, *ibid.*, 230.

[8]) A. Robertson and A. Plummer, *A Critical and Exegetical Commentary on the First Epistle of St. Paul to the Corinthians* (ICC; Edinburgh, 1914), 200.

[9]) G. Heinrici, *Kritisch exegetisches Handbuch über den ersten Brief an die Korinther* (Meyers kritisch exegetischer Kommentar über das N.T.; Göttingen, 1888), 272.

[10]) P. Bachmann, *Der erste Brief des Paulus an die Korinther* (Kommentar zum N.T. ed. T. Zahn; Leipzig, 1921), 330.

[11]) E. Schweizer, *TWNT*, VI, 435.

[12]) Neuenzeit, *op. cit.*, 49.

terminology for the Eucharistic elements (cf. Didache 10, 3), [1]) is rejected by Neuenzeit [2]) (and rightly we think, but not for his reason) because this technical terminology would not be known as such to the Corinthians. However it seems that the main reason for rejecting such a meaning here is Paul's overall attitude toward the Israel of old. Considering his attitudes in Rom 7—8, is it conceivable that he would maintain the wilderness generation was given the Spirit? And should we grant this possibility, then why does Paul never say so?

As for the second meaning, "figurative, prophetic," the main analogy for this usage is Apoc 11, 8, and the main reason for claiming this meaning here is the presumed relationship of this passage to the Eucharist. Now there are two difficulties with this interpretation. In the first place, the interpretation of the drink as referring to the blood of Christ seems a bit forced; after all the drink of the Israelites was water. In the second place, most of the exegetes cited above, and not only those who hold that "spiritual" here means figurative, prophetic, believe this passage in Paul refers to O.T. analogies for the Christian sacraments of Baptism and the Eucharist. To us this seems a gratuitous assumption. As the text stands, it is meant to be a Scriptural proof related to 1 Cor 9, 27: "but I pommel my body and subdue it, lest after preaching to others I myself should be disqualified"; cf. γάρ in 1 Cor 10, 1. And the whole point of the rabbinic Scriptural proof in 10, 1-11 is to point up the *kelal* principle in v 12 ("Therefore let the one who thinks he stands fast watch out lest he fall"), which is a variant of the same idea expressed in 9, 27 — which is what Paul set out to prove in the first place. The *kelal* principle in turn is directed to the "all things are lawful" group in Corinth and their attitude toward idolythites. Hence the primary aspect under Paul's consideration is a comparison between the situation of the wilderness generation and the situation of the Corinthian "all things are lawful" group. [3]) Whether Paul intended all the items mentioned in his

---

[1]) Goppelt, *TWNT*, VI, 146.

[2]) Neuenzeit, *loc. cit.*

[3]) Emphasized by Neuenzeit, *op. cit.*, 47; L. Goppelt, "Paulus und die Heilsgeschichte: Schlussfolgerungen aus Röm IV und I. Kor. X. 1-13," *NTS* 13 (1966/1967), 33 maintains: "I. Kor. x erklärt entgegen einem mysterienhaft-magischen Missverstehen der Sakramente vom hellenistischen Synkretismus her, dass der Gemeinde in den Sakramenten Gottes Heilshandeln ebenso unentrinnbar und doch unverfügbar begegnet wie Israel in der Wüste." This judgment is much conditioned by what one considers the nature of the Corinthian community to have been; if the community were more Jewish than Gentile, the problem may have been one of "Jewish syncretism," and have nothing at all to do with

Scripture proof and its conclusions (10, 1-10) to correspond to identical items in the experience of the Corinthian community (e.g.
baptism in Moses = Christian baptism; spiritual food and drink =
Eucharist; desire, idolatry, fornication, testing God, murmuring =
identical sins in the Corinthian group) is possible, but need not be
so at all. After all, his purpose is to prove his *kelal* principle. And
if he chose to use the experience of the desert generation as his proof,
what other benefits and what other sins could he possibly mention
which he did not.

As for the benefits, he lists the cloud, the passage through the
sea, the manna and the well. For a man of his rabbinic training,
Paul's omission of the gift of the Law seems unpardonable, except
for his attitude toward the Law in view of the coming of Christ. Yet
in our passage, Paul does seem to have had the Law in mind, and
to have done precisely what we would have expected, i.e. substitute
Christ for the Law. In rabbinic tradition, the well either was the Law
or imparted the Law. Thus in the Damascus Document, we find the
following exegesis of Nb 21, 18: " 'the well which princes dug, which
the nobles of the people delved with the staff.' The Well is the
Law." [1]) And Mekilta on 13, 17 offers the following tradition: "I will
lead them out into the wilderness for 40 years, so that they might
eat the manna and drink the water of the well, and thus the Torah
will be assimilated by their body." [2]) What Paul does here, then, is
substitute Christ for the Law, a procedure quite understandable for
Paul since in his view, the "law" aspect of the Scriptures has come to
an end in Christ.[3])

Finally, if Paul intended "spiritual" to mean "figurative, with a
view to the Christian sacraments," then why did he not use this
adjective for the cloud and the sea? Be that as it may, it is quite certain
that Paul's main intention here is not to contrast O.T. sacraments
with N.T. sacraments. And therefore "spiritual" would not pri-
marily mean "(pre-)figurative, prophetic."

The third meaning of "spiritual" indicated above is "heavenly, of

---

the Christian sacraments here; cf. J. M. Ford, "The First Epistle to the Corinthians
or the First Epistle to the Hebrews?," *CBQ* 28 (1966), 402-416.

[1]) CDC VI, 3-4 cited from C. Rabin, *The Zadokite Documents* (Oxford, 1958), 22.

[2]) H. S. Horovitz (ed.) with I. A. Rabin, *Mechilta d'Rabbi Ismael cum variis
lectionibus et adnotationibus* (Corpus tannaiticum III/1; Frankfurt, 1931), 76.

[3]) Cf. B. Gerhardsson, *Memory and Manuscript: Oral Tradition and Written
Transmission in Rabbinic Judaism and Early Christianity*, trans. E. J. Sharpe (Acta
Seminarii Neotestamentici Upsaliensis 22; Lund-Copenhagen, 1961), 283 ff.

divine origin." By far this meaning is the most obvious and satisfying. Neuenzeit accepts it as meaning "deriving directly out of God's world and bestowing God's power," and maintains that any further interpretation of the word would go beyond what the text is really saying.[1]) The exegetes holding this interpretation generally derive it from the phrase "spiritual food"; since spiritual food means the mana, and the manna is called "the bread of heaven, bread of angels" (Ps 78, 24 f.) or "food of angels" (Wis 16,20), therefore "spiritual" means of heavenly origin, supernatural in origin. Consequently, the word "spiritual" in the rest of the passage has the same meaning as it does in the phrase "spiritual food."

The value of this interpretation is that such usage is also witnessed to in early Christian literature, namely II Clement 14, 1.2.3.5. In this passage from II Clement,[2]) the author speaks of the Church and Christians; he writes:

v 1: ἐσόμεθα ἐκ τῆς ἐκκλησίας τῆς πρώτης τῆς πνευματικῆς, τῆς πρὸ ἡλίον καὶ σελήνης ἐκτισμένης.

v 2: καὶ ἔτι βιβλία καὶ οἱ ἀπόστολοι τὴν ἐκκλησίαν οὐ νῦν εἶναι, ἀλλὰ ἄνωθεν· ἦν γὰρ πνευματική, ὡς καὶ ὁ Ἰησοῦς ἡηῶν . . .

Thus in this usage, "spiritual" connotes "from above," or "from the beginning" (ἄνωθεν), hence of heavenly origin with the formal nuance of pre-existent.

Now this seems to be precisely the meaning in our Pauline passage; and Paul himself seems to indicate it by the explanation he appends to the phrase "spiritual drink" in v 4. In other words, instead of beginning with "spiritual food" to find the meaning of the word "spiritual," we ought begin with "spiritual rock" and Paul's explanation of it.

Paul informs us that all the Israelites of the wilderness generation drank the same spiritual drink precisely because (γάρ) they used to drink of the spiritual rock that followed them, and this rock was the Messiah, the Christ. Paul thus clearly tells us that Christ was

---

[1]) Neuenzeit, *op. cit.*, 49: "Hier geht es nur darum, diese Speisen von den natürlichen zu unterscheiden; sie sollen charakterisiert werden als Gaben, die 'direkt aus Gottes Welt stammen und Gotteskraft schenken' (citing Schweizer, *TWNT*, VI, 435). Jede weitere Interpretation überfordert den Stellenwert." However it seems equally beyond what the text says to maintain that "spiritual" means "Gotteskraft schenkend," because this would be tantamount to "giving pneuma," an interpretation which Neuenzeit forcefully rejects. He further suggests a paraphrase as "vom Gottesgeist gewirkt" or "erfüllt," but even this seems to go beyond the text.

[2]) Cited from F. X. Funk, *Opera Patrum Apostolicorum* (Tübingen, 1887), I, 160.

with the wilderness generation, that the Messiah was pre-existent. Now if the spiritual rock was Christ, then the rock too was pre-existent, i.e. of heavenly origin, hence spiritual. The food too would be spiritual in this sense, i.e. of heavenly origin, pre-existent. Thus πνευματικός here, like in II Clement, denotes "spiritual" with the connotation of "from above, pre-existent." Hence the word "spiritual" here formally means "from above, pre-existent."

What Paul does here is employ the exegetic traditions current in his day. That both the well [1]) and the manna [2]) were created at the beginning in heaven, and there reserved for the Israelites of the desert wanderings is well known from the PT and other sources contemporary with Paul. Whether Paul was directly dependent on the Targums for this information is impossible to say; rather it seems more probable that he picked up this information, including the exegetical tradition of the wandering well or rock, in the course of his studies in Beth Hillel.

In conclusion, then, it would seem that the word "spiritual" in our text has the formal connotation of "from above, pre-existent." Thus what Paul has in mind here is the pre-existent manna, wandering well and Messiah, all of which came down from above to benefit the wilderness generation.

2) *Apoc* 2, 17

In the message to the Church of Pergamum, the seer of Patmos delivers the following promise:

"To the victor I will give some of the hidden manna . . . "
Our purpose in this sub-section is to determine the origin of the hidden manna, and more specifically, the attribute "hidden," κεκρυμμένον.

A frequent opinion among exegetes is that "hidden manna" refers to the jar full of manna put up before the Ark (Ex 16, 32); the Ark and its contents were hidden (2 Mac 2, 4) only to reappear in Messianic

---

[1]) Cf. P. Grelot, " 'De son ventre couleront des fleuves d'eau,' la citation Scripturaire de Jean VII, 38," *Revue Biblique* 66 (1959), 369-374; R. Le Déaut, "Miryam, soeur de Moïse, et Marie, mère du Messie," *Biblica* 45 (1964), 198-219 for PT texts and rabbinic references; cf. also the following note.

[2]) Cf. 56 ff. above; on Paul and the PT, cf. M. McNamara, *The New Testament and the Palestinian Targum to the Pentateuch* (Analecta Biblica 27; Rome, 1966), 70-96; 168-188; 246-252; 254-255.

times [1]) (thus substantially Moffat,[2]) Ramsay,[3]) Swete,[4]) Allo,[5]) Boismard,[6]) Prigent [7])). Zahn [8]) objects to this view since the O.T. records that the Tabernacle was plundered by Israel's enemies at an early date; for him the hidden manna is Jesus (he refers to Jn 6) after his Ascension and now hidden. Both the foregoing views are rejected as unwarranted by Charles [9]) and as early as Düsterdieck[10]) as well. Wikenhauser[11]) does not give an opinion on the origin of the term "hidden manna," but agrees in the main with both Charles and Düsterdieck on the significance of this reward — a symbol of intimate fellowship with God in eternal life. Moreover, Charles holds the "hidden manna" is simply the heavenly manna of the O.T. and the Sibylline Oracles (VII, 148 f. = which is post N.T.); while Düsterdieck says the manna is "hidden" because it will be revealed only in future glory. Finally, Bonsirven[12]) states that "hidden" means set aside, reserved, and the hidden manna would be like the other extraordinary foods destined for the happiness of the world above. In general, therefore, there are three opinions on the phrase "hidden manna": (1) the jar of manna in the Ark, to be restored in Messianic times; (2) the heavenly manna of the O.T., also to be restored in heaven, in eternal life; or as Oepke[13]) has it, this O.T. manna is now

---

[1]) For the rabbinic sources, cf. L. Ginzberg, *The Legends of the Jews* (Philadelphia, 1928), VI, 19, nn. 111-112; the oldest form of this tradition derives from R. Eliezer (90-130 AD) in Mekilta on Ex 16, 32.

[2]) J. Moffat, *The Revelation of St. John the Divine*: in W. R. Nicoll (ed.), *The Expositor's Greek Testament* (London, 1910), V, 358.

[3]) W. M. Ramsay, *The Letters to the Seven Churches of Asia and their Place in the Plan of the Apocalypse* (London, 1904), 308.

[4]) H. B. Swete, *The Apocalypse of St. John* (3d ed.; London, 1922), 38.

[5]) E. B. Allo, *Saint Jean: l'Apocalypse* (EB; Paris, 1921), 29.

[6]) M. E. Boismard, *L'Apocalypse* (Bible de Jerusalem; Paris, 1950), 33.

[7]) P. Prigent, *Apocalypse et Liturgie* (Cahiers Theologiques 52; Neuchatel, 1964), 20.

[8]) T. Zahn, *Die Offenbarung des Johannes: Erste Hälfte* (Kommentar zum N.T. ed. T. Zahn; Leipzig, 1924), 274-275.

[9]) R. H. Charles, *A Critical and Exegetical Commentary on the Revelation of St. John* (ICC; Edinburgh, 1920), I, 65-66.

[10]) F. Düsterdieck, *Kritisch exegetisches Handbuch über die Offenbarung Johannis* (Meyers kritisch exegetischer Kommentar über das N.T.; Göttingen, 1887), 164-165.

[11]) A. Wikenhauser, *Offenbarung des Johannes* (Regensburger N.T.; Regensburg, 1947), 38.

[12]) G. Bonsirven, *L'Apocalisse di San Giovanni*, trans. U. Massi (Verbum Salutis; Rome, 1963), 111.

[13]) A. Oepke, *TWNT*, III, 977.

hidden in the sense that it will be revealed in eschatological times;
(3) the manna reserved for the elect in the world to come.

None of the aforecited authors makes reference to the PT, and yet
it seems that the PT Ex texts best explain what the author of the Apocalypse had in mind. In the first place, he did not have the jar of
manna in mind since all the rewards offered to those who conquer
(Apoc 2, 7.11.26; 3, 5.12. 21) are in heaven or the after life; hence also
the hidden manna (and white pebble) of 2, 17. Now both in biblical
tradition (2 Mac 2, 4) and rabbinic tradition (cf. 100, n. 1 above)
the jar is hidden on this earth. As for the second opinion, that the
manna is "hidden" because not apparent now, the author of Apocalypse does not seem to have this in mind because all the other
rewards are equally "hidden" now, yet none of them are called
"hidden." We might add here that those championing this second
opinion (Charles, Düsterdieck and Wikenhauser), while incorrect on
the meaning of "hidden," are correct in referring this gift to heaven,
a spatial metaphor for the world to come, rather than eschatological
times, a temporal metaphor; for in his list of rewards, the author
of the Apocalypse consistently uses spatial images (2, 7.26; 3, 5.12.21).
As for the final opinion (Bonsirven), it seems precisely what the
author of our passage did have in mind, i.e. "hidden" = reserved,
set aside. And this is precisely the meaning the phrase "hidden
manna" would have if it were derived from an exegetical tradition
as that preserved in the PT.

As a matter of fact, in speaking of the "hidden manna" as a reward
for the victor, our author seems to have combined two traditions. The
first would be that of the manna hidden away by God from the beginning in heaven (and hence still there; there is no tradition, either
in the O.T. or in rabbinic writings, to the effect that the manna
ceased to exist in the realm from which it originated); this tradition
is preserved in the PT.[1]) The second would be a tradition similar to
the one handed on by R. Eliezer b. Ḥasama (ca. 110 AD): "In this
world (בעולם הזה) you are not going to find it (the manna), but in
the world to come (לעולם הבא) you are going to find it." [2]) The
image again is spatial, and most probably refers to heaven.[3]) Be

---

[1]) Cf. also TJI and TJII Gen 4, 24 on the tree of life of paradise, pre-existent
and now preserved in the world to come לעלמא דאתי and Apoc 2, 7; on the
Apocalypse and the PT, cf. McNamara, *The N.T. and the Palestinian Targum*,
97-125; 189-237; 256.

[2]) Mekilta on 16, 25 (Horovitz, 169).

[3]) Ginzberg, *The Legends of the Jews*, VI, 17, n. 97 indicates that לעולם הבא in

that as it may, it seems certain that the author of the Apocalypse was dependent upon the PT or a tradition similar to the one preserved in the PT for his idea of the hidden manna.

3) *Jn* 6, 31 *ff*

The manna figures prominently in the homiletic midrash [1]) in Jn 6, 31-58, commonly known as the Bread of Life discourse. The problem is why the mention of the manna at all; why does John (or Jesus) make reference to the manna at this point in the gospel. The most feasible solutions to this problem to date are those deriving from the fact that this chapter states that the Passover was near ·(v 4) and that this discourse took place when Jesus taught in synagogue (v 59). Basing himself on these references, Gärtner [2]) views the ancient Jewish Passover practices, especially the Passover lections and the Passover Haggada as the overall background for the mention of the manna here. The difficulty with this view is that the manna is not especially prominent in the Passover Haggada, and the "formal parallels," adduced by Gärtner, between this Haggada and the Bread of Life discourse are not parallel at all.[3]) However Gärtner's reference to the Passover-tide lections as background of this discourse is probably correct.

Guilding,[4]) on the other hand, approaches the whole of John's

the aforecited Mekilta text means heaven—a spatial image, hence used inaccurately here; he writes: "In view of the statement in PK 5, 49b and BR 48.10, one is inclined to assume that in the Mekhiltas the expression לעולם הבא is used inaccurately instead of לעתיד לבוא i.e. the messianic times." Billerbeck, *Kommentar*, IV, 794, shows no such doubt; he writes: "Mit ʿOlam ha-ba kann gemeint sein das Jenseits (Welt der Seelen) aber auch die messianische Zeit, u. endlich noch die zukünftige Welt im engeren Sinn, d.h. die Zeit der Endvollendung nach Ablauf der Tage des Messias."

[1]) After the work of P. Borgen, *Bread from Heaven* (Supplements to Novum Testamentum X; Leiden, 1965), 28-98, it seems certain that this is the literary form of Jn 6, 31-58; the problem is whether the homily is based on a Pentateuch verse or on a proem text as A. Finkel thinks in *The Pharisees and the Teacher of Nazareth* (Arbeiten zur Geschichte des Spätjudentums und Urchristentums IV; Leiden, 1964), 158-159.

[2]) B. Gärtner, *John VI and the Jewish Passover* (Coniectanea N.T. 17; Uppsala, 1959), 14 ff., 25 ff.

[3]) As pointed out, e.g. by R. Brown, *The Gospel according to John I-XII* (The Anchor Bible 29; New York, 1966), 266-267; there are more than four questions in the Bread of Life discourse, hence no parallel with the four questions of the Passover Haggada.

[4]) A. Guilding, *The Fourth Gospel and Jewish Worship: a Study of the Relation of St. John's Gospel to the Ancient Jewish Lectionary System* (Oxford, 1960), 60 ff.; the calendar is on 234.

gospel from the point of view of the triennial lectionary cycle in use in Palestine in the first century. The problem with Guilding's suggestion relative to Jn 6, 31-58 is that she bases her lectionary cycle on a calendar which cannot be definitely proved to have been in use in the first century.[1]) Moreover, even granting that the calendar in question was in use, all the texts Guilding cites as background for the Bread of Life discourse occur after the Passover in that calendar, some as much as a month after.[2]) And even if we grant that these post-Passover texts were actually in use at the time specified, why would Pentateuch texts telling of the crossing of the Red Sea and the gift of the manna be "the two miracles . . . that would be most appropriate for Passover-tide and the theme of Jesus' sermon." [3]) These texts would be equally "most" appropriate for the feast of Unleavened Bread, which would fall much closer to the time when the texts alleged by Guilding were to be read, than they would to Passover time.

Yet while Guilding and Gärtner do not offer a satisfactory solution, we believe they are both correct in pointing to a relationship between the Bread of Life discourse and the synagogue lections during the time of John (or Jesus). Hence as far as our passage in John is concerned (i.e. prescinding from Guilding's thesis of a lectionary cycle for the whole of John), the problem remains as to precisely what synagogue reading did John (or Jesus) have in mind that made

[1]) For a criticism of Guilding's work, cf. L. Morris, *The New Testament and the Jewish Lectionaries* (London, 1964); we are interested only in what Guilding has to say about the Passover lections and Jn 6.

[2]) Guilding, *op. cit.*, 61 writes: "The lections we must consider, then, are those for the second half of Nisan, especially those for the last Sabbath in that month: Gen 6, 9 ff; Ex 15, 1 or 22; and Nb 11." However in the hypothetical calendar on p. 234, Gen 6, 9 ff is listed as the reading for the first week of Iyyar, while Ex 16 on the gift of the manna (a text to which Guilding refers later on this page) is listed for the first two sabbaths of Iyyar. Further, Guilding says: "A clue to the link between the accounts of the giving of the manna in Ex 16 and Nb 11 and the seder for the first year of the cycle, Gen 3, is given in the remark in Midrash Sifre on Nb 11, 7 . . ." (p. 62). The remark she quotes alludes to Gen 2. Finally, as for the haphtarah read with Gen 6, 9 ff., Guilding notes that this haphtarah was Is 54, 9—55, 5 (thus indicating that Jn 6, 45—which cites Is 54, 13—as well as Jn 6, 27.63—dependent upon Is 55, 2 — would have been influenced by this haphtarah), "a passage which all authorities agree in allocation as haphtarah to Gen 6, 9" (p. 63). However, as noted by A. Büchler, "The Reading of the Law and the Prophets in a Triennial Cycle. II," *Jewish Quart. ·ly Review* 6 (1894), 42: "All authorities agree in attaching Is. 54, 9-10 as Haftara t ، Gen 6, 9 since the Flood and Noah are expressly referred to in these verses"; not the Passover!

[3]) *Ibid.*, 61.

mention of the manna, thus offering an occasion for the homiletic midrash in Jn 6.

On this point, we should like to suggest that perhaps John (or Jesus) was influenced by a Targum to Josh 5, much like the one preserved in the MS fragment cited above (pp. 77-81). Reasons for this suggestion are not lacking. In the first place, Josh 5 was certainly an ancient Passover haphtarah, probably in use in the first century (cf. 83 f. above). Secondly, Josh 5 is the only O.T. text linking the manna with the death of the desert generation, an idea repeated in Jn 6, 49.58, and much emphasized in the targumic MS fragment. The MS fragment also makes mention of the murmuring theme which was part of the O.T. manna tradition and referred to in Jn 6, 41.43. If such a Targum were the background of the Bread of Life discourse, it would also explain the echo of Nb 21, 6-9 in Jn 6, 35-40; this O.T. passage is referred to explicitly at the beginning of the MS fragment and seems to be intimated by Jn 6, 35-40:

| Jn 6, 35: hunger and thirst [1]
39: Jesus loses nothing
40 (36): see Jesus and
believe = life | Nb 21, 6: no food, no water
7: many people die
9: see the raised serpent
and pray/turn one's
heart to the name of
YHWH's Memra (cf.
PT Nb 21, 9 [2])) = life |

And finally, if a targumic tradition like the MS fragment were the background for Jn 6, 31 ff., the adapted citation of Is 54, 13 would be an argument by John (or Jesus) against the primacy of the Torah in MS fragment Tg Josh 5, 14-15; Jesus takes the place of the Torah as the argument developed in Jn 6 from Is 54 shows. Naturally, this suggestion is hypothetical; but it certainly is no worse than the many hypotheses already advanced relative to the Bread of Life discourse.

On the other hand, it is certain that the idea of the manna as "coming down, sent down." — an idea preserved through the PT tradition — is at work in this discourse. Once the manna motif was

---

[1] Brown, *The Gospel according to John I-XII*, 272-273, among others, sees in this verse a reference to sapiential themes in the discourse; this, of course, is possible, but it seems simpler to relate this verse to the manna tradition. Besides, given the style in the discourse, how else would the author express total satisfaction in the area of eating than in the way the verse does.

[2] Cf. M. E. Boismard, "Les Citations targumiques dans le quatrième évangile," *Revue Biblique* 66 (1959), 374-378, especially 378.

chosen as an element in the discourse, the fact of its "coming down," of "being sent down" fitted in perfectly with John's understanding of the Christ-event in vertical dimensions rather than horizontal historical dimensions.[1]) The contrast here is between the manna which came down or was sent down but could cause no transformation in those who partook of it in spite of its heavenly origins, and Jesus who came down or was sent down and could transform those who partook of him and endow them with life.

With the homily of Jn 6, the midrashic treatment of the manna tradition beginning in the O.T. and running through the PT, reaches its Christian terminal in the N.T. corpus. The homily most probably uses some Passover-tide synagogue lection as a springboard. The ideas bound up with the manna referred to in the homily certainly derive from the manna motif as preserved in Palestinian exegetical tradition. And the homily certainly has the literary form of an early rabbinic midrashic sermon. As a conclusion to our study of the manna tradition, we might ask what distinctive light does the use of the homiletic midrash form throw on the manna — food of death — and Jesus — the bread of life. To answer this question we shall review the salient features of midrash as described by Bloch[2]) and compare these with Jn 6, 31 ff.

First, the point of departure of rabbinic midrash is Scripture; it is a reflection upon the sacred texts, a "research" into the meaning of the texts. The same holds true for the homily in Jn 6; its point of departure is the text quoted from Scripture by Jesus' hearers. In Jn 6 the manna tradition is meditated upon in the light of Jesus.

Second, rabbinic midrash is of a homiletic character; its origin is certainly to be sought mainly in the liturgical reading of the Scriptures on Sabbaths and feast days. John tells us Jesus "spoke these things while teaching in synagogue in Capharnaum" (v 59); hence given the literary form of Jn 6, 31 ff., a liturgical reading of the Scriptures ought certainly be the background of the homily.

Third, rabbinic midrash is an attentive study of the text, employing all possible means to shed light upon obscurities in the passages commented upon. Every effort is made to explain the Bible by the Bible, as a rule not arbitrarily, but by exploiting a theme. In John, the endless repetition of the words of the text under consideration (v 31b)

---

[1]) Cf. R. H. Smith, "Exodus Typology in the Fourth Gospel," *JBL* 81 (1962), 333; P. Benoit, "Paulinisme et Johannisme," *NTS* 9 (1962/1963), 205.

[2]) R. Bloch, "Midrash," *DBS*, V, cols. 1265-1266.

throughout the homily evidences punctilious analysis (and not various sources, we might add). On the other hand, there is no attempt to explain the Bible by the Bible, but to explain the Bible by the person of Jesus. This is quite logical since for John, Jesus is the fulfillment of and substitute for the Torah, the living Word of God (cf Jn 1). And the procedure in our homily is not arbitrary; rather the theme is uniform, the bread of life.

Fourth, rabbinic midrash has a thoroughly practical scope, to adapt the Biblical message to the present; midrash is an up-dating of the Scriptures. In Jn 6, this is precisely what John (or Jesus) does — adapt the manna motif to the new situation, to the new religion "in spirit and truth" (Jn 4, 23). In line with John's double perspective method of handling time,[1]) the manna motif is contrasted with the need of Jesus' contemporaries to believe in him for life eternal, as well as with the need of the post-Resurrection Church to understand what the Eucharist is really about.

Fifth, and finally, according to the character of the Scriptural text being commented upon, rabbinic midrash either seeks to clarify the legislative texts with a view to solving problems not dealt with in the Bible (= halaka), or it seeks to unravel the true meaning of the narratives and the events of Israel's history (= haggada). In the homily in Jn 6, both the text commented upon and the questions put to Jesus indicate it is obviously a question of haggada, to find the true meaning of the event mentioned in the Scriptural passage, i.e. the manna event. According to the exposition in our homily, the manna of tradition falls short on all counts in comparison with Jesus, the bread of life.

Thus what we have in Jn 6, 31 ff. is a Christian midrash on the manna tradition, a meditation on this tradition in the light of Jesus, an explanation of the true meaning of this tradition in terms of Jesus, an up-dating of this tradition called forth by the fact that the Word became flesh.

---

[1]) The Johannine trait of viewing two time-perspectives simultaneously has been pointed out by E. Haenchen, " 'Der Vater, der mich gesandt hat'," *NTS* 9 (1962/1963), 214; he calls it "Ineinssetzung."

BIBLE, TARGUM, APOCRYPHA, PHILO AND JOSEPHUS, RABBINICS

* refers to footnote

INDEX II

PERSONAL NAMES

* refers to footnote

Abba b. Papa, 82*
Abbuha, 66*
Abrahams, I., 59*
Aḥa, 87*
Akiba, 73, 85
Allo, E. B., 95, 100
Alonso-Schökel, L., 6*, 7*
Ammi, 68
Anan, 84*
Aphraates, 88*
Aquila, 67
Assi, 68
Auzou, G., 20*

Bachmann, P., 95
Barth, C., 16*, 25*
Benoit, P., 105*
Berekiah, 90*
Beyerlin, W., 17*
Billerbeck, P., 59*, 69*, 88*, 102*
Blau, L., 69*
Bloch, R., 17*, 42*, 43*, 86*, 87*, 105*
Boismard, M. E., 100, 104*
Bonsirven, J., 100 f.
Borgen, P., 53*, 61*, 88*, 102*
Brekelmans, C., 5*
Brockington, L. H., 76*
Brown, R., 102*, 104*
Buchanan, G. W., 77*
Büchler, A., 83, 103*
Buxtorf, J., 55*, 57*, 61*

Catford, J. C., 54*
Cazelles, H., 1*, 17*, 18*, 21
Charles, R. H., 100 f.
Clement of Rome, 98 f.
Cohn, L., 72*, 90*, 91*
Coppens, J., 1, 2*, 9*, 10*, 23

Danby, H., 51*
Daube, D., 88*
Díez Macho, A., 43*, 50*, 77*
Dosa, 89*
Driver, S. R., 25*
Düsterdieck, F., 100 f.

Eissfeldt, O., 20*, 21, 22*, 23, 25*, 26, 37, 91*
Eleazar b. Azariah, 87
Eleazar of Modiᶜim, 53*, 59*, 61, 62*
Eliezer, 60, 62*, 100*
Eliezer b. Ḥasama, 101
Epstein, I., 61*

Fichtner, J., 76*
Findlay, G. G., 95
Finkel, A., 52*, 102*
Ford, J. M., 97*
Freedman, H., 57*
Friedmann, L. M., 84*

Gärtner, B., 102 f.
Geiger, A., 64*, 66*
George, A., 27, 30*
Gerhardsson, B., 52*, 97*
Ginzberg, L., 57*, 60*, 61*, 65, 69*, 82*, 85*, 88*, 100*, 101*
Goldin, J., 72*
Goppelt, L., 95 f.
Gray, G. B., 21 ff.
Gray, J., 17*
Grelot, P., 99*
Guilding, A., 62*, 102 f.
Guttmann, A., 69*

Haenchen, E., 106*
Heinrici, G., 95
Herrmann, W., 35*, 39*

Irenaeus, 88*
Ishmael, 52, 73*, 85
Israelstam, J., 57*

Jastrow, M., 56*, 57*, 60*, 65*
Jaubert, A., 18
Joḥanan, 60*, 72*, 82
Jose, 73*
Jose b. Ḥanina, 66*
Jose b. Judah, 90*
Josephus: see previous index
Joshua, 60*, 62, 90*
Josiah, 58